S0-DSF-707

YOUR RETIREMENT

How to Plan for a Secure Future

Action for Older Persons, Inc.

Cynthia L. Page, Editor

ARCO PUBLISHING, INC.
NEW YORK

Published by Arco Publishing, Inc.
215 Park Avenue South, New York, N.Y. 10003

Copyright © 1984 by Action for Older Persons, Inc.

All rights reserved. No part of this book may
be reproduced, by any means, without permission
in writing from the publisher, except by a
reviewer who wishes to quote brief excerpts in
connection with a review in a magazine or
newspaper.

Library of Congress Cataloging in Publication Data
Main entry under title:

Your retirement.

   Includes bibliographical references.
   1. Retirement—United States.   2. Retirement.
I. Page, Cynthia L.   II. Action for Older Persons, Inc.
HQ1063.Y68   1984   646.7′9   84-2820
ISBN 0-668-05945-1 (Paper Edition)

Printed in the United States of America

10 9 8 7 6 5 4 3 2

Contents

Acknowledgments

This book is based upon *PREP for Your Future*, a group-discussion preretirement education program prepared and sponsored by Action for Older Persons, Inc. (AOP). AOP is a nonprofit planning and advocacy agency, funded in part by the United Way of Broome County, New York. As one of its services, AOP conducts training seminars and designs materials for organizations that wish to offer retirement planning programs to their employees, members, or the general public. Over twenty thousand people have participated in the PREP program across the United States and Canada.

Action for Older Persons developed PREP with funds from the New York State Office for Aging, the Federal Administration on Aging, and the Florence and John Schumann Foundation. AOP has served as an advocate of preretirement education since it first produced and marketed PREP in 1974.

Assistance in creating this new work was generously provided by many people, including Peter G. Beatty, Valerie S. Nixon, Chandler Y. Keller, and Francis Battisti. Particular recognition must also go to the AOP Board of Directors, Michael M. Perhach, President; the PREP Advisory Committee, Jon Erion, Chairman; and the AOP Office Staff, Kristen Mason, Virginia Haworth, and Margaret Lounsberry.

AOP is also indebted to all its members for their continued support and to the people who have participated in the various PREP seminars and helped us advance preretirement education.

A special thanks to Johnny Hart and Field Enterprises, Inc., for allowing us to use the delightful B.C. and Wizard of ID cartoons.

Finally, Cynthia Page, AOP Assistant Director, is the person truly responsible for this book in its final form. Cindy has instilled her vitality and spirit into this project throughout its evolution. Her many hours of research, writing, and rewriting, and her endless good humor have given us all something special to keep and remember.

RICHARD NASSAU
Executive Director
Action for Older Persons, Inc.
Binghamton, New York

Introduction

"There is nothing either good or bad, but thinking makes it so."
—Shakespeare

Retirement. The word prompts bleak visions for some—loss of job and the status attached, reduced income, and vast idle time. But for many others retirement means new opportunities, a time to refocus activities, pursue forgotten dreams, even start a new business or second career!

The keys to enjoying retirement are understanding and planning for what lies ahead, and it's never too early or too late to begin. The chapters that follow cover a wide range of retirement concerns. Not all the topics will be of equal importance to you at this time. But remember, life brings constant change and the various possibilities explored in this work may become important at some future time.

We have begun each chapter with a warm-up quiz that previews the material to follow. Throughout the text of each chapter are planning tools and charts to aid you in developing your personal retirement plan. Concluding each chapter are "situations" that act as examples or "what ifs" exploring some common yet underplanned-for challenges in retirement. So sharpen your pencil, get comfortable, relax, and begin planning your retirement dream.

Chapter 1
Opportunities and Adjustments in Retirement

CHAPTER 1 WARM-UP

Before reading "Opportunities and Adjustments in Retirement," test your general knowledge of the subject by placing a check mark next to the answer you prefer. Check the key at the end to find the correct answer.

1. As much as one third of one's life may be lived in retirement.   True_____ False_____

2. Successful retirement depends mostly on: luck_____ attitude_____ money_____ planning_____

3. Most people identify themselves by their job role.   True_____ False_____

4. Housewives never retire.   True_____ False_____

5. Your ability to adjust to change at age seventy will be similar to your ability to adjust at age forty.   True_____ False_____

6. Most older adults feel life in retirement is better than they expected it to be.   True_____ False_____

7. Most people have negative expectations of old age.   True_____ False_____

8. "Senility" is a natural part of the aging process.   True_____ False_____

9. The majority of older adults are working or would like to have some kind of work to do (including household and volunteer work).   True_____ False_____

10. Most older adults have no interest in, or capacity for, sexual relations.   True_____ False_____

Key: 1. (T), 2. Planning, 3. (T), 4. (T), 5. (T), 6. (T), 7. (T), 8. (F), 9. (T), 10. (F).

THINKING ABOUT RETIREMENT

Two generations ago many more people lived on farms and continued to work as long as they were able to do something useful. Now most people live in metropolitan areas, and when they reach their sixties are expected to retire from their jobs. People grow older today just as they did two generations ago, but with one difference. Then they had a fairly good idea of what was going to happen during their later years. Now the question facing many thousands of retiring Americans is, Retire to what?

We know nowadays what to expect of children when they first go to school, of young people who are taking their first job and getting married, and of adults who are making a living and rearing a family. But there are no generally accepted rules for people to follow when they change from a working to a retirement way of life. No wonder, then, that those approaching retirement are asking questions, such as:

- What can I do with my time when I stop working?
- Are there ways to be useful after retirement?
- How can I make sure that life will be secure during the retirement years?

Most people face these issues squarely and with a great deal of courage; and, fortunately, most create a satisfactory way of life after retirement. Nevertheless, experience shows that retirement can result in misgivings, feelings of uselessness, and low morale. How people react to retirement usually depends on how well they understand what is going to happen and how well prepared they are to handle the situation.

When we decide, or are required, to relinquish lifelong habits of work, earning a living, and raising a family, we sometimes have difficulty achieving a new equilibrium. Studies show that occupational retirement removes a base from which people derive personal satisfaction and social identity. Moreover, retirement from work often means a drastic reduction in income and a vast increase in leisure time. We may be completely unprepared to use this time in ways that yield the same satisfaction and social usefulness as did our employment. Poor health and decline in energy reserves often aggravate the situation, as does the need to adapt long-standing marital arrangements when a

retired couple begins to spend twenty-four hours a day in the home together.

The rapidly increasing numbers of active, capable, and longer-living older persons are challenging the outmoded stereotyped ideas of how people should spend their retirement years. Retired people are no longer willing to accept the inactivity, loss of identity, and even rejection that retirement has meant in our culture. They are aware that they have much to offer and are demanding significant roles in society.

RETIREMENT STEREOTYPES

In the minds of many people retirement is a time of idleness, uselessness, and rapid mental and physical decline. Let's take a look at these stereotypes one at a time.

Do retirees have too much time on their hands? Are they bored? Undoubtedly some are. But many retired people report that they have more to do than ever before, and indeed more than they have time for. Boredom is a serious problem in retirement, but one that you must deal with yourself. Some people already have an idea of what they want to do with their spare time in retirement, but many have not given it much thought. One thing is for sure: Interesting and rewarding activities will not just magically appear after you retire. You may look on retirement as a time of welcome inactivity after a busy career, but most find that they can take only a few weeks or months of this before boredom sets in. And numerous studies, combined with reports of the experiences of those who have retired, show that those who are most active are those who are healthiest and happiest.

Are retirees useless? The commonly accepted definition of retirement is to be no longer working for a living. However, this doesn't mean retirement from life. Working for a salary or wages is only one way to feel useful. In retirement we still remain important to our family and friends, and many retirees have become involved in endeavors that are both tremendously rewarding to themselves and of much value to society.

It should also be remembered that quite a few retirees continue to work on a part-time basis, or develop some other income-producing sideline. Again, feelings of uselessness are something that only you can do something about. Anticipating now what your situation may be can help you plan for an interesting and useful retirement.

Does retirement mean physical and mental decline? One man, retired for several years, announced proudly one day that he had made it. When asked what he meant by this he replied that he had read that many people die within three years of retirement. He had just passed the three-year mark and felt he was therefore out of the danger zone. Perhaps it's good for us to keep two things in mind in this regard. One is that retirement and old age are not necessarily synonymous. While it is true that during our retirement years we grow older, many people retire during middle age. The other is that aging and poor health do not necessarily go hand in hand. In the chapter on health in this manual we distinguish between aging and illness, and provide specific ideas to help prevent sickness from interfering with enjoyment of retirement. Now, before retirement, is the time to closely examine ways in which you can take an active and important role in ensuring your good health.

Aging by itself will probably have little or no effect upon you as a person. If you've always been an active, vital, and optimistic sort of person you will

remain so in your later years. Similarly, the "crotchety old man or woman" in late adulthood was most likely a crotchety younger person, unhappy with his or her life and self from early years. In short, the changes or problems encountered in aging will affect you as those you've experienced previously have affected you.

RETIREMENT MEANS CHANGE

Retiring from work is one of the major mileposts in life, ranking in importance with marriage, parenthood, and the beginning of employment in the way that it alters everyday living. More than anything else, retirement means change. Changes in retirement can be external, related to such things as moving to a new location, having less money to spend, or having greater amounts of time to spend on a hobby. Changes can also occur inside you, such as how you feel about your new status, or the effect on your mood of having less responsibility because you are no longer working. In many ways these internal changes may be more important than the external ones, because they have such an influence on how much you are able to enjoy life.

Of course, for some people the changes are more drastic than for others. A two-thousand-mile move to a retirement community, for example, is quite a bit more of a change in circumstances than staying in the same home and community after retiring. And change has a greater effect on some people than on others. Each of us has different abilities to adapt to new situations.

Those who have studied retirement indicate that, generally speaking, people react to and deal with changes brought on by retirement in much the same way they have dealt with other changes throughout life. If, for example, you handled your "mid-life crisis" without too much trouble, the chances are you will do all right in retirement as well.

The impact that changes have on you, however, can be greatly influenced by how much you can anticipate those changes, and by how much time and effort you put toward preparing yourself.

Some things don't change. As an older adult you will need the same basic things you've always needed: dignity, money, adequate health care, and a useful and satisfying way to spend your time. Without proper planning it's unlikely these basic needs will be satisfied in retirement. So now is the time to begin working on obtaining and securing your basic needs.

RETIREMENT MEANS CHOICE

When you set goals based on anticipated needs and changes, you can identify the actions you need to take now to achieve your goals. Remember, you will need to review your plans on a regular basis as the future can never be fully foreseen and planned for. But you can certainly sweeten the odds of successful retirement through proper preparation.

Comprehensive planning for retirement can have a number of advantages:

- It will give you a clearer idea of what lies ahead. You can take a detailed look at various options in areas such as housing and finances.
- It will increase your ability to influence and control your retirement years, so that you do not merely react to the circumstances in which you find yourself.
- It gives you time to "try on" the feeling of being retired. You can gradually grow accustomed to the idea of retirement.
- It gives you time to come up with practical ideas to deal with problems you might confront in retirement.
- It helps you identify goals years ahead of time and take the necessary steps to assure that you reach them.

How Do You Really Feel About Retiring?

This is really one of the key questions you should ask yourself now. Do you put off thinking about it, or feel too uneasy or anxious when you do consider what it will be like? It's helpful to know that a high percentage of people feel this way.

Many people look to retirement with feelings of both optimism and worry. This is true of those who retire voluntarily as well as those who are forced to retire by company policy or because of their health, and by those who retire early as well as by those who retire at the traditional ages. If you anticipate

B.C.   by johnny hart

PLANNING TOOL

To get a clear idea about how you presently feel and what your plans are now with regard to retirement, complete the following:

1. I plan to retire in _____ years.

2. The idea of retiring makes me feel (place an "X" on the line)

   _____

   very depressed   no special feeling   terrific

3. I feel the way I do about retirement because

4. For me, the single most important thing to know about my retirement is

5. The part of my job that I'll miss most in retirement is

6. The biggest change I expect in retirement is

7. The thing I look forward to *most* in retirement is

8. The thing I look forward to *least* in retirement is

9. Areas that I need to pay particular attention to in preparing for retirement are:

   _____my health   _____where I will live
   _____legal affairs   _____spending my money
   _____finding satisfying things   wisely
   to do   _____talking things over
   _____where my retirement   with my spouse
   income will come from   _____
                                      _____

10. Three things I really want to do in retirement are:
    (1)
    (2)
    (3)

retirement this way, planning and taking a close look at retirement can help minimize the worry you feel and increase your feelings of optimism. And there's no doubt about it—your attitude toward retirement will heavily influence the degree of satisfaction you gain from it.

AGING AND RETIREMENT

What is it like to be a "senior citizen"? Will I feel any different? Will people treat me differently? What will I do with my free time? Do I really want to retire? These are the kinds of questions we need to address when thinking about and planning for our retirement.

In the minds of many people, aging and retirement are synonymous. In fact, they are quite different. Retirement is something that happens at a certain time in our life. All of our life is devoted to growing, becoming, and aging.

The term "older person" is altogether relative. To a ten-year-old, a teenager is an older person. To a sixty-year-old, someone ninety is an older person. We ourselves are all older people—older than we were a year ago, and older than many other people are.

As we grow older, changes take place within us and outside of us. We can't reverse these changes, even if we want to. But we can deal with them and happily adjust to our own aging.

According to the National Council on Aging, it is not the young alone who have negative expectations of growing older. Older adults themselves believe the stereotypes and myths of old age; and, when they recognize that life is not so bad for them, consider themselves to be the exception to the rule.

In fact, for many older adults, life has turned out better than they expected it to. For every older person who feels that his or her life is worse now than what he or she thought it would be, there are three who say that life is better now than they expected. In fact, as many younger adults feel their current lives fall short of their expectations as do those sixty-five and over.

People do, however, sometimes experience undue and harmful anxiety because of images they have about growing older or because of social attitudes toward older adults. When you look at yourself in a mirror and see your hair graying or skin wrinkling, you might think of yourself as less attractive. When the mass media equate romance, vitality, and energy with youth, you might think of yourself as over the hill. Or when you are looking for a job and are discriminated against because of age, you might feel that you have nothing more to contribute.

It is time to put those false and hurtful misconceptions and misportrayals aside. By the year 2000 about one third of the country's population will be over age forty-five. And the year 2000 is not far away. How old will you be?

"Remaining Life Expectancy"

Below is a chart depicting the average life span for "anyone," regardless of sex, race, economic conditions, etc.

Current Age	Average Years
45	31.9
50	27.6
55	23.5

Current Age	Average Years
60	19.7
65	16.3
70	13.1
75	10.4
80	8.1
85	7.6

So if you are now forty-five it is likely you will live to age seventy-seven. Once you've reached age seventy-seven it is then likely you will live to age eighty-seven and so on. Theoretically, the outer limit of the human life span is 120 years.

Let's face it, we all have a vested interest in changing society's and our own concepts of aging if we are to plan successfully for all aspects of a long and good life.

ADJUSTING TO GROWING OLDER

How can we deal with our own aging and with changes that accompany aging? For sure, we can't drink from any magical fountain of youth. But we can adjust, adapt, and continue to be creative, purposeful, involved, and happy.

In terms of our physical capabilities, learning to do things a little more slowly as we grow older makes a lot of sense. Shoveling snow, lifting heavy objects, and climbing stairs are among the areas where slowing down is important. But a decline in physical strength does not mean withdrawing from active work. It only means not pushing ourselves beyond our natural limits.

Besides adjusting physically to growing older, there are other things we can do that are equally important. Here are five of them:

- We can try to broaden our range of interests. There's a wise saying that goes, "It's not good to put all your eggs in one basket." Having a wide variety of interests helps make life more exciting and brings us into contact with more people and experiences. If for some reason we become unable to do one or two things that we have enjoyed, we will still have the benefit of having many other interests.
- We can try to make new friends and to keep in contact with old friends. Because of moving, or death, or for other reasons, we lose people who had been close to us. Taking the time to build new friendships is an important element in our continuing enjoyment of life and in our own mental health.
- We can recognize the times when we need help. Throughout our lifetime, things happen to us for better or for worse. When they happen for the worse, we often need not only the support of friends but also the assistance of professionals and the services of a community. Knowing when such help is needed is not a sign of weakness, but of good sense. If there are problems that we cannot get out of our mind, or needs we have that are not being satisfied, getting help may be the best answer.

- We can resist the labels that people tag us with and the boxes they want to put us in. We are what we are. And we are what we make of ourselves. We should be offended when people describe us as less capable than we are, or when they treat us as if we were "over the hill." We are experienced, mature people and should expect and even demand that we be treated that way.

We can look for courage and strength within ourselves to deal with life's experiences and our own aging. In the last analysis, it is the vitality of our own spirit that makes or breaks our life. That vitality is nourished by varied interests, good friends, recognition by others, and outside help. But it is not the same as all those things. There is a reservoir of strength within ourselves that we ourselves can and need to tap if our life is to be as full and satisfying as possible. It is that vitality that provides the basis for adjusting to new situations.

ADJUSTING TO RETIREMENT

There is no doubt that some important social and emotional adjustments must be made when retiring, regardless of one's age. Many find it extremely helpful to take a close look at what these adjustments might be well before they retire, so they have some idea of what to expect and can work on ways to deal with changes that occur.

In one sense, we have all had some experience with retirement. Each time we change our circumstances in life, we retire from one role only to begin another. We retire from being students; perhaps we retire from single life, or from childlessness. We also may retire from parenthood to some degree when our children become adults. Each of these changes signals a change in our role in relation to the world outside us and carries with it some internal adjustments in the way we see ourselves.

Earlier, we said that aging was a gradual process, taking place throughout our lives. Retirement, on the other hand, can be seen in two ways. One way is that it is an event occurring at a particular point in time. On a certain day, we officially become "retired" and our status is changed from that point in time. Another way of thinking of retirement is that it is a period of time in our lives, covering perhaps many years, and possibly interrupted by periods of employment.

What will you miss most about your job when you retire? A Louis Harris survey commissioned by the National Council on the Aging found that it was often not the work itself but the income and the people at work that were most dearly missed.

The amount and difficulty of adjustment to retirement seems to be related to several factors. One of these is the importance of the work role in our overall identity. Some people are able to make the shift from satisfaction through paid employment to satisfaction from other activities. Others, however, are not able to accomplish this easily. It may be because they are too tied up in their work, or because they never took the time to really explore other areas that might be of interest to them.

Another factor related to adjustment in retirement is financial security. Studies show that those who retire with too little income are less satisfied with retirement overall. This reinforces the importance of financial planning well before we retire.

A third factor seems to be the number and diversity of interests an individual has. It has often been said that you can't fish, bake, play golf, or sew every day. For most people, no single activity or interest will provide lasting satisfaction.

Our task is to anticipate how we will react to retirement and to predict what forces will be influencing us. Steps can be taken then to see that we continue to satisfy our needs to feel secure, to be creative, to have contact with our friends, to be valued as a person for our contributions, and to have a purposeful and satisfying life.

Retirement for women not formerly in the work market will mean that they will probably continue doing what they have always done as homemakers and housewives. But retirement planning is nonetheless valid, as the return of a spouse to the house, either full- or part-time, will require personal planning and adjustments to adapt to this new phase of life.

For working women, adjustment to retirement will be as difficult as it is for their male counterpart, and proper preparation is just as vital.

RETIREMENT AND MARRIAGE

Marriage, especially one that has lasted over a long period of time, connotes sharing and intimacy. Marriage in retirement can take on an even greater role in fulfilling social and emotional needs. In fact, many couples reach their peak of marital satisfaction during their retirement years together.

To achieve this harmonious marital state, two things seem to be fundamental. One is open and frequent communication and the second is the mutual respect of each spouse for the other.

Jokes are often heard about retired husbands who are bossy and constantly in the way when their wives are trying to get things done around the house. Unfortunately, the jokes often reflect real life. There is no doubt that adjustments need to be made on both sides in such situations. Husbands need to realize that they can't simply barge in and expect to direct their spouse's work routines because they know a "better way." Wives must realize that their husbands have time on their hands—perhaps more time than they know what to do with—and may be experiencing strong emotions related to their recent retirement.

There are other situations that husbands and wives may have to deal with in relation to retirement. One such is the case of the two-career family when one spouse decides to or must retire before the other. Should she voluntarily retire when he does? Or vice versa?

Marital adjustments in retirement usually are accomplished without too much difficulty, but anticipating them and talking together about feelings, plans, and expectations can do much to enhance retirement.

SINGLE RETIREMENT

Retirement can pose special problems and opportunities for the single person. Single adults with few family commitments or "significant others" who are dependent on them can be lulled into a false sense of unaccountability. Single adults have just as great a need to plan for a successful retirement as their married counterparts.

Though single people often have fewer financial commitments to deal with during their working years, there will probably be a heavier financial burden on them in retirement because of a lack of family resources (both financial and other supportive services) to draw upon. For example, if a disability occurs a single adult may have additional expenses for housekeeping, shopping services, and the like that a couple may not need to incur.

For single persons who do not need to consider in their daily routines the plans or wishes of someone else, the habit of acting independently may become harder to focus constructively to fill the vast hours of newly acquired free time in retirement. Proper planning will again assist in structuring a retirement life-style. Singles usually possess traits of positive determination and self-reliance that equip them well for finding creative and new ways to spend this time. And indeed the freedom and habit of doing as one pleases can open many doors to new experiences and reduce the stress of joint decision-making and change often felt by retiring couples.

A TIME-PLANNING TOOL

	YES	NO
Have you begun to plan for the extra hours of free time you will have in retirement?		
Are you interested in working either part-time or full-time in a second career?		
Are you currently active in any of the following organizations?		
Church group		
Social club		
Service club		
Charitable organization		
Study group		
Professional group		
Community advisory board		
Other _____		
Do you plan to join or continue to be involved with any of the above organizations in retirement?		

	YES	NO
How many of these things do you do now and do you think you will continue to do in retirement?		
Work around the house	_____	_____
Work in garden	_____	_____
Work on a hobby	_____	_____
Watch television	_____	_____
Attend sporting events	_____	_____
Play sports	_____	_____
Attend movies	_____	_____
Attend club meetings	_____	_____
Attend theater, concerts, lectures	_____	_____
Play cards or other games	_____	_____
Read regularly	_____	_____
Take courses	_____	_____
Other _____	_____	_____
What new things do you plan to do in the future?		
Learn a new skill	_____	_____
Become a volunteer worker	_____	_____
Travel	_____	_____
Take courses	_____	_____
Learn a new sport or game activity	_____	_____
Develop a new hobby	_____	_____
Join a new organization	_____	_____
Does your spouse share many interests with you, and do you participate in them together?	_____	_____
Do you have an active social life with friends or relatives?	_____	_____

ACTIVITIES IN RETIREMENT

Adjustment to and satisfaction in retirement are closely related to activities engaged in during that time. But what are some typical activities enjoyed by retirees? Just as with other adults, retirees choose activities that satisfy a variety of needs, including relaxation, excitement, a feeling of contribution, income, physical activity, group participation, intellectual stimulation, and creativity.

Generally speaking, the activities retired people engage in can be divided into the following categories:

- Group membership activities—church, community, and neighborhood groups; service clubs.
- Hobbies and recreation—sports, craftwork, travel, social activities, education.
- Volunteer work.
- Home and family activities.
- Employment.

Throughout our lives we belong to various groups, both on a formal and an informal basis. For many, group participation is an important part of social or religious life. The need to be part of a group is just as great in retirement as it was earlier. In fact, when we retire we may feel a greater need to be part of a group, to make up for the loss of social contact and feeling of acceptance we formerly received in our place of work.

Retired people have found a great deal of satisfaction and have contributed much through involvement in church groups, service clubs, neighborhood organizations, political parties, and volunteer fire departments.

In most communities there are well-developed networks of senior citizen clubs and centers eager for your participation. Most clubs meet on a weekly or monthly basis and are privately run by their members. Senior centers, on the other hand, are usually places where people can go every day to participate in a variety of activities, such as craftwork, card playing, exercise classes, dancing, and educational programs. In addition, many senior centers offer nutritionally balanced hot meals at very reasonable prices, and help keep you informed of programs and services available in the community.

More than anything else, senior citizen clubs and centers offer opportunities to make friends and to feel a part of what is going on. And the importance of friendships should not be overlooked. Everyone needs someone with whom they can share their private feelings, and someone who can be counted on when problems arise. This is just as true in retirement as in other periods of life.

Many communities contain organizations established especially to further the interests of their older populations. The success of such advocacy groups often depends on membership dues and the active participation of the members. Volunteer work of retired people is valuable because they help a great deal in showing the community the value of its older citizens, in identifying the needs of older people, and in helping to plan appropriate programs to meet those needs.

Studies of voting behavior have consistently shown the same pattern: low voter participation among the youngest age group (18–24); a steady increase to a peak in the forties and fifties; and a gradual decline in the sixties and seventies. However, those seventy-five and over still vote more frequently than those in the youngest age group.

Voting is just one form of political participation. Dissemination of general knowledge of current events; work in a political party; and active participation in local politics are all areas where older adults tend to play a leading role.

The following are addresses of two national-level organizations concerned with the well-being of retired and older people:

National Council of Senior Citizens, Inc.
1511 K Street, N.W.
Washington, DC 20005

American Association of Retired Persons/National Retired
    Teachers Association
1909 K Street, N.W.
Washington, DC 20049
(may have a local chapter in your community)

Experienced retired people are quick to point out that no single activity can provide a satisfying life in retirement. No one denies, however, that hobbies and recreation add richness and enjoyment to life. Regardless of whether your interest is travel, sports, craftwork, or education, it shouldn't be difficult to find others with similar interests. There are clubs and associations for almost any special interest you can name, from license plate collecting to African violets to bicycling. To find out about these you need only ask around, pick up a magazine related to your particular interest, or check in the telephone book. Most such groups are eager for new members.

In these days of rising fuel costs, travel can be expensive, especially if done by private automobile. There are ways to get around this, however, by using other forms of transportation and by taking advantage of off-season rates, senior citizen discounts, and package and group tours. Many bus companies, airlines, hotels, and taxicabs offer substantial discounts to senior citizens during certain seasons or days of the week. Many senior clubs or centers organize and sponsor group-travel packages which offer added bonuses of traveling with friends and increased social activities.

There are a number of sports in which retired people participate and which require varying degrees of skill. Retired people are involved in almost all noncontact sports. The chances are, if you become involved in a sport it will be one in which you have had a long-time interest. But don't be afraid to try something new. One of the big advantages of retirement is being able to use the tennis courts, bowling alleys, campgrounds, and golf courses during the week, while others are working. Before starting any sport that requires even moderate physical activity, be sure to check with your physician.

If over the years you have developed skill in a particular craft, you may want to offer some of what you do for sale. In most areas there are a number of craft shows each year where you can display and sell your goods. Even if you don't plan to sell your work, you can save substantially on your gift-giving by making many presents—and the gifts will have more meaning, too.

In greater numbers than ever before, retired and older people are found on America's college campuses and in the classrooms. There is a renewed interest in education among retired people. At the same time, because of declining enrollments, schools and colleges are actively courting mature students.

In some areas, older people can attend classes free, with no special educational background needed. In such cases the older students sit in on regularly scheduled classes, but are not required to do homework or take exams, unless credit toward a degree is desired.

In addition, short, noncredit courses on topics ranging from health to current events to hobbies and crafts are becoming very popular among retired people. To find out more about such opportunities in your area contact the continuing education department at a nearby high school, community college, or university, or call the local Cooperative Extension office.

ELDERHOSTEL is a network of several hundred colleges and universities in all fifty states and Canada, which offers special low-cost, one-week residential academic programs for older adults. Most programs are scheduled during the summer months. Programs normally begin Sunday evening and end Saturday morning. Cost is all-inclusive for room, board, tuition, and extracurricular activities. For more information write: ELDERHOSTEL, 100 Boylston Street, Suite 200-E, Boston, MA 02116.

Many communities are fortunate in having volunteer recruiting organizations. The Voluntary Action Center, which recruits people of any age for various kinds of volunteer service, is one such agency. Another is the Retired Senior Volunteer Program (RSVP), which provides opportunities for retired people to serve the community. Here are a few other possibilities that may be available in your community:

- Assisting in the public schools.
- United Way Campaign.
- Working for a political candidate or party.
- Meals on Wheels—preparing or delivering meals to homebound people.
- Friendly visiting in hospitals and nursing homes.

If you are unsure of how to take advantage of one of these opportunities, contact your local Area Agency on Aging.

Volunteer/Work Programs

Several of the most popular volunteer/work programs are run under the sponsorship of ACTION, a federal agency. Your expenses for participation in the ACTION programs are paid. For individuals in a low-income bracket there are the Foster Grandparent and Senior Companion Programs that offer a small salary. For more information on ACTION programs, write ACTION, 806 Connecticut Avenue NW, Washington, DC 20525, or call your operator and ask for the toll-free ACTION phone number for your area. The following are ACTION programs:

- **Peace Corps**—Peace Corps volunteers work in developing foreign countries, teaching in technical and nontechnical fields including education, agriculture, health, and engineering. Volunteers serve a two-year, full-time stint, receive training in the language and culture of the country in which they will serve, and receive a financial readjustment allowance for each month of service when they return to the United States, as well as reimbursement for their expenses while abroad. In recent years, larger percentages of Peace Corps volunteers have been older adults than ever before. If you have a talent or skill to share and want to see foreign lands as an insider rather than as a tourist, the Peace Corps could be for you.

- **VISTA** (Volunteers in Service to America)—VISTA is the domestic counterpart of the Peace Corps, working in social services, education, health, housing, community planning, and economic development to help fight poverty. Volunteers serve full-time for one or two years, after a three- to five-week training period. VISTA furnishes housing, living allowances, personal expenses, and a financial readjustment allowance for each month of service at the end of your commitment. Older Americans are becoming an increasingly large segment of the VISTA ranks.

● **RSVP** (Retired Senior Volunteer Program)—The RSVP Program calls for a part-time commitment within your own community, and is open to anyone age sixty or over. The services provided in each location vary widely according to need but include such things as assistance to educational institutions, health care facilities, and various human service organizations.

● **Foster Grandparent Program**—Volunteers spend twenty hours each week providing love, friendship, and companionship to troubled children in hospitals and institutions. The program is open to adults over the age of sixty with low incomes and offers a modest salary. Training in counseling children is provided.

● **Senior Companion Program**—Similar in requirements and payment to the Foster Grandparent Program but aimed at serving the needs of the frail elderly.

Another exceptional volunteer organization, not under the ACTION program, is SCORE (Service Corps of Retired Executives) for retirees, which is designed to provide you with the opportunity to share your skills and experience by helping struggling new or young business operators. For more information contact your local Small Business Council or the national office at 1441 L Street NW, Washington, DC 20416.

TIME-PLANNING TOOL #2: A TYPICAL WEEK

One of the most stressful aspects of retirement can be waking up in the morning and having nothing to do all day. Try planning a "schedule" for a typical week in your retirement.

	SUNDAY	MONDAY	TUESDAY	WEDNESDAY	THURSDAY	FRIDAY	SATURDAY
Morning							
Afternoon							
Evening							

WORKING AFTER RETIREMENT

Retirement from a job doesn't necessarily mean retirement from work altogether. Large numbers of people retire from the organization for which they have worked for years, only to look for and find other employment, either full-time or part-time. Those with skills in certain areas are often in demand because younger workers have not had the time or inclination to develop similar abilities.

A number of communities, recognizing the value of older workers, have established organizations for the purpose of bringing together older workers looking for employment and businesses and industries seeking to hire mature workers. And more employers are recognizing the value of these workers. In contrast to the popular myth of older workers as slow and inefficient, recent studies show that, in most situations, they are just as valuable as when they were younger. Older workers have been shown to be more dependable, to take fewer sick days, to be more apt to report to work on time, and to have a better accident record than their younger counterparts.

Increased numbers of employers are providing flexible work/retirement options including the following:

- Reduced work schedules (three- or four-day weeks) prior to retirement
- Increased vacation time in years prior to retirement
- Retired employee consultant programs
- Temporary or permanent part-time work programs for retirees.

Generally, these options allow for increased choice as to the time of retirement and provide for various forms of continued employment.

What Kind of Job Is Right for You?

There are job opportunities for older adults in both government and private industry. The following list suggests part- and full-time jobs that many retirees successfully perform. You may want to match them against your experience, aptitudes, and desires as a guide for the kind of second career you might enjoy. Most important, don't be self-conscious. Tell your former employers, relatives, friends and acquaintances, the members of your clubs, fraternal or political organizations, or church that you are looking for work. A large percentage of workers get jobs that way.

If you like to deal with the public:

- Salesperson.
- Real estate sales.
- Waiter or waitress.
- Travel agent.
- Information clerk.

If you like to work with numbers or in an office:

- Receptionist.
- Typist.
- Retail cashier.
- Tax advisor.

If you like to work outdoors:

- Landscaper.
- Farm assistant.
- Service station attendant.
- Deliveryman.

If you have interests in the arts:

- Musician or artist.
- Freelance writer or editor.
- Tutor.
- Antique dealer.
- Manager of a bookstore, flower shop, and so on.

If you're good with your hands:

- Auto mechanic.
- Carpenter.
- Painter or paperhanger.
- Tailor or seamstress.
- Beautician.
- Cook or caterer.

Tips for Mature Job Seekers

In the employment of older adults there is no more influential person than the individual job seeker. Obtaining a job frequently means adjustment on the part of the applicant to changes in work, in pay, in working conditions, and so on.

These tips may help you as a mature job seeker, but it is not intended to be complete. For more information contact your local State Employment Service. Some states provide special programs and services to aid older adults in finding employment. There is no charge for this service.

DO

Stress your qualifications for the job opening.

Recount experience you have had that would fit you for the job.

Talk and think, so far as possible, about the future rather than the past.

Indicate, where possible, your stability, attendance record, and good safety experience.

Remember that older employees are capable, dependable, trainable, careful, and steady.

Try to learn ahead of time about the company and its products.

Assume an air of confidence.

Approach the employer with respectful dignity.

Try to be optimistic in your attitude.

Maintain your poise and self-control.

Try to overcome nervousness or shortness of breath. (It helps to take a deep breath.)

Hold yourself erect.

Apply for a specific job or jobs.

Answer questions honestly and straightforwardly.

Stress the contribution you can make to the enterprise.

Have available a list of former employers, with dates and period of service.

Apply for the job in person.

DO

Let as many people as possible know you are job hunting.

Know the importance of getting along with people.

Recognize your limitations.

Make plenty of applications.

Indicate your flexibility and readiness to learn.

Be well groomed and appropriately dressed.

DON'T

Keep stressing your need for a job.

Discuss past experience that has no application to the job situation.

Apologize for your age.

Be untidy in appearance.

Display "cocksureness."

Cringe or beg for consideration.

Speak with muffled voice or indistinctly.

Be one of those who can "do anything."

Hedge in answering questions.

Express your ideas on compensation, hours, etc. early in the interview.

Hesitate to fill out application, give references, take physical examination, or tests on request.

Hang around, prolonging interview, when it should be over.

Go to an interview without a record of your former work connections.

Arrive late and breathless for interview.

Be a know-it-all or person who can't take instructions.

Depend upon the telephone for your job.

Isolate yourself from contacts who might help you find a job.

Feel that the world owes you a living.

Make claims if you cannot "deliver" on the job.

Display a feeling of inferiority.

A Sample Outline for Preparing a Resume

A resume is a printed picture of what you have to offer an employer. It can be mailed out or hand-delivered to prospective employers with a cover letter, or can serve as your organized fact sheet in an interview.

    I. Heading (precedes all other data)—name, address, telephone.
   II. Occupational Interest and Goal—the kind of job you want. If several, list them in order of preference.
  III. Work History—can be done two ways: A, by job; B, by function.
       A. By Job—list in inverse chronological order: dates of employment; employer; address; nature of business; name and title of supervisor; position you held; job duties—emphasize those highest skilled and special equipment used; scope of responsibility—how many/much you supervised and to whom you were responsible; accomplishments—any outstanding results with facts, figures.
       B. By Function—list by broad fields in order of their importance to your job/goal objective. For example: Public Relations, Sales,

other, with previous job experience and accomplishments for each of the fields.
IV. Military Experience (if any)—length of service, branch of service, duties performed (details of any in desired job field).
V. Education
    A. Graduate Schools—major, degree, and date received.
    B. College—major, degree, and date received.
    C. High School—do not include if you have a higher degree.
    D. Other successfully completed training programs.
    E. Extracurricular activities.
VI. Miscellaneous Information—Languages: speaking, reading, writing ability. Special skills: typing, drive car, experience from volunteer or other activities. Professional contributions and achievements: publications, memberships in organizations, etc.
VII. Personal Data (optional)—date of birth, citizenship, health, marital status, dependents.

Starting Your Own Business

The United States Small Business Administration lists these characteristics an individual should have before attempting to start his or her own business:

- Initiative.
- Positive attitude.
- Leadership and organizing ability.
- Industriousness.
- Responsibility.
- Ability to make quick and accurate decisions.
- Sincerity.
- Perseverance.
- Consistently high level of physical energy.

Another useful asset would certainly be luck. Starting a small business can be a very difficult task. Approximately 20 percent of all small businesses fold before the end of their first year, and only half survive for three years. Lack of management ability, inadequate capital, improper purchasing, improper marketing, and poor location are among the major causes of small-business failure.

You can succeed in small business, however, if you prepare yourself thoroughly, take courses, read books, get experience, ask questions, know your business and your market thoroughly, and set reasonable, reachable goals. It's also important to talk to your lawyer about the legal form your business should take.

Starting Fresh, or Buying a Franchise or Existing Business?

Starting fresh with a new business certainly permits you the most freedom, since you are not restricted by what has gone before and are not regulated by someone else's rules. On the other hand, there are distinct advantages to buying an established franchise or an existing business.

In the case of a franchise, the purchaser or franchisee receives the right to operate a business under the leadership of a well-known distributor or manufacturer. In return for a fee and royalty payments, the franchisee has immediate access to a proven product, a consumer image, publicity, and goodwill. In many instances, the franchisor provides the goods—be they automobiles or fried chicken—as well as the training and techniques for conducting the operation. If the franchise is a sound one, the likelihood of success in one's own business is increased.

There are, however, disadvantages to franchises: You have to conform to the chain's standards, sell only their product at their price, share in the problems of the distributor though they may be none of your doing, perhaps find that centralized management is unresponsive to your needs, and, of course, share the profits.

If you are considering buying a franchise, you should visit other franchisees, the Better Business Bureau, and the Chamber of Commerce to investigate the company's reputation and track record. Before you sign any contract you should consult your lawyer, since your agreement will regulate such key items as exclusivity, inventory, royalty rates, purchase requirements, and investment obligations.

The great attraction of entering business through a franchise is that all the planning comes prepackaged for the franchisee, often at a far lower price than if he or she were to start fresh. This avoids the problem of raising large sums of money—the most difficult part of establishing a business.

Buying an existing business also simplifies the matter of capital formation: You must negotiate a price on terms satisfactory to both parties. In general, however, it requires more money to buy a business than to start one. The worth of an enterprise is more than its book value, or the sum of its assets less its liabilities: it has also developed a following, customers, trade relations, management efficiency, public acceptance—in short, goodwill. A prospective buyer must be ready to compensate the owner for all the intangible efforts that go into building a thriving business.

The third factor to consider in buying a business, in addition to book value and goodwill, is the ability of the enterprise to earn money. In order to understand its earnings, one should look at the record for the last three to five years. Businesses are often bought and sold on the basis of their earnings alone, but it is wise to consider book value and goodwill along with the earning potential.

In buying an ongoing business you have some of the same advantages as a franchise: an active and loyal clientele, a known product or service, goodwill, and all the past efforts that went into making the business successful. But there may be a different set of disadvantages. Why is the previous owner selling? Are there any impending changes in the nature of the business or in the character of the neighborhood? Most important, what is the extent of the company's liabilities? What promises or contracts has the company entered into that might commit the new owner in the future? The danger of hidden liabilities when buying an established business is a strong reason for starting out fresh with your own business.

The Small Business Administration (SBA) has over a hundred local offices. To find the office in your city, look in the telephone directory under "U.S. Government, Small Business Administration." The SBA has a great number of brochures and fact sheets on all aspects of small business. The Starting and Managing Series is available at a nominal charge.

PLEASURABLE ACTIVITIES QUESTIONNAIRE

Both now and in retirement don't forget to set aside time for the simple everyday pleasures of life. A review of this checklist may remind you of pleasures you've lost the time for and inspire you to take the time to please yourself more often. The rewards for such simple pleasures are improved mental, physical, and emotional health.

Following is a checklist developed by Dr. Lillian R. Dangott, *A Time to Enjoy: The Pleasures of Aging*. "For the older person, as for everyone, pleasurable experiences are a necessity. Intelligent pleasure, along with the search for life meanings and ethical living, provide the substance for health and the energy to live. To spice up life with pleasure is as important as to season our food. When you enjoy life, you cherish it more."

	Compared to 5 years ago, I enjoy this activity			I wish that this activity would occur			Check if not applicable
Creative or Self-Expressive Activities	Less	Same	More	Less	Same	More	
1. Growing houseplants							
2. Redecorating my house or office							
3. Working in the yard or garden							
4. Working with my hands: sewing, knitting, needlework							
5. Playing, singing, or arranging music							
6. Photography							
7. Being in a play							
8. Doing creative art work such as painting, designing, sculpture, moviemaking							
9. Craft work, such as making jewelry, pottery, leather, beads, weaving							

	Compared to 5 years ago, I enjoy this activity			I wish that this activity would occur			Check if not applicable
Creative or Self-Expressive Activities	Less	Same	More	Less	Same	More	
10. Collecting, such as stamps, coins, shells, rocks							
11. Finding a new hobby							
12. Doing creative writing: poetry, stories, plays							
13. Writing letters, cards, diary, or journal							
14. Cooking, baking, or canning							
15. Woodworking, carpentry, auto-mechanics							
16. Fixing or repairing things							
17. Doing housework, making things clean							
18. Other:							
Activities Involving the Giving of Service to Others							
1. Donating something for a good cause							
2. Working in politics							
3. Joining a new organization							
4. Being active in community service projects—religious, charitable, or volunteer work							
5. Being an officer in an organization or club							
6. Being an active member in an organization or club							
7. Listening or advising on problems							
8. Other:							
Work- or Job-Related Activities							
1. Working at my trade or profession							
2. Doing something useful							
3. Being appreciated for my work							
4. Feeling important							
5. Getting status							
6. Having something to do							
7. Getting paid; being financially independent							
8. Playing "hooky" from work or school							
9. Other:							

Activities of Social Involvement: Family, Friends, Community	Compared to 5 years ago, I enjoy this activity			I wish that this activity would occur			Check if not applicable
	Less	Same	More	Less	Same	More	
1. Talking or writing about old times—my personal past							
2. Talking about my health or my problems to someone who cares							
3. Eating out							
4. Having a picnic							
5. Being with my family							
6. Being with children							
7. Spending time with friends							
8. Remembering a departed friend or loved one; visiting the cemetery							
9. Long conversations on the telephone							
10. Finding a new friend or lover							
11. Dating, courting, or flirting							
12. Going to or giving parties							
13. Entertaining friends at home							
14. Going to church functions							
15. Going to a bar, tavern, nightclub, floorshow							
16. Hitchhiking, or picking up a hitchhiker							
17. Having a good conversation							
18. Being recognized as sexually attractive							
19. Sharing humor; having a good laugh							
20. Shocking people, swearing, or flaunting different ideas for the fun of it							
21. Saying "no" to someone's request							
22. Directing or organizing people to do something							
23. Knowing that I am appreciated or needed—getting "stroked"							
24. Other:							
Sports or Athletic Activities							
1. Water Sports: Swimming, surfing, snorkeling, scuba diving, boating, sailing, canoeing, water skiing							
2. Earth Sports: Hiking, camping, rock climbing, fishing, kite flying							
3. Animal Sports: Bird watching, horseback riding, dog training, other activities with animals							

	Compared to 5 years ago, I enjoy this activity			I wish that this activity would occur			Check if not applicable
Sports or Athletic Activities	Less	Same	More	Less	Same	More	
4. Individual Competition Sports: Wrestling or boxing, bowling, Frisbee, tennis, archery, fencing, badminton, horseshoes, golf, pool or billiards, table tennis							
5. Team Sports: Football, soccer, hockey, baseball, softball, basketball, volleyball, and the like							
6. Air Sports: Piloting, gliding, parachuting							
7. Snow Sports: Skiing, sledding, snowmobiling							
8. Jogging or very fast walking							
9. Gymnastics							
10. Doing exercises fairly regularly							
11. Doing yoga							
12. Bicycling or motorcycling							
13. Ice skating or roller skating							
14. Going dancing							
15. Other:							
Spectator Activities							
1. Watching TV or listening to the radio							
2. Going to a sporting event							
3. Going to movies or plays							
4. Going to an X-rated movie							
5. Other:							
Contemplative and Spiritual Activities							
1. Listening to records or music tapes							
2. Making time to be alone; enjoying solitude							
3. Reading the Scriptures							
4. Attending church							
5. Talking to God							
6. Hearing a good sermon							
7. Saying prayers							
8. Meditating							
9. Other:							
Being With Nature							
1. Listening to nature's sounds, such as the wind in the trees							

	Compared to 5 years ago, I enjoy this activity			I wish that this activity would occur			Check if not applicable
Being With Nature	Less	Same	More	Less	Same	More	
2. Looking at the sky, clouds, storms, stars, sunrise, sunset							
3. Looking at flowers, plants, and trees							
4. Taking a drive into the country							
5. Walking or driving in the mountains							
6. Being at the ocean							
7. Spending time outdoors enjoying nature							
8. Going for a walk							
9. Other:							
Sensuous or Self-Pleasuring Activities							
1. Being barefoot; feeling the earth with my feet							
2. Sunbathing; feeling the sun's warmth							
3. Sitting and thinking; daydreaming							
4. Napping							
5. Going without clothes, nude							
6. Singing or humming							
7. Buying something for myself							
8. Sleeping late in the morning							
9. Waking up early in the morning							
10. Masturbating							
11. Getting "high" on marijuana							
12. Having a drink or two							
13. Smoking							
14. Going to a spa or sauna bath							
15. Taking a hot, leisurely bath							
16. Going to a gym or health club							
17. Getting or giving a massage or back rub							
18. Other:							
Educational Activities							
1. Going to a museum, exhibit, or library							
2. Learning something new							
3. Doing experiments or other scientific work							
4. Reading educational literature (technical, professional)							
5. Learning or speaking a foreign language							

	Compared to 5 years ago, I enjoy this activity			I wish that this activity would occur			Check if not applicable
Educational Activities	Less	Same	More	Less	Same	More	
6. Attending lectures, seminars, or taking a class							
7. Attending a concert (opera, dance, ballet, or rock festival)							
8. Other:							
General or Nonspecific Pleasurable Activities							
1. Traveling							
2. Visiting a zoo, circus, or amusement park							
3. Exploring; hiking or walking in new places							
4. Gambling or betting							
5. Going to garage sales							
6. "People-watching"							
7. Planning vacations							
8. Reading for entertainment, such as a newspaper or novel							
9. Other:							

When was the last time you had "fun"? _____

_____

_____

_____

What were you doing? _____

_____

_____

_____

As you look back over the activities that you wish you did more frequently (column 2 of "Pleasurable Activities Questionnaire"), what reasons prevent you from doing so? _____

_____

_____

_____

_____

_____

What kinds of things or activities do you do to relieve stress? _____

_____

_____

_____

_____

SITUATIONS TO CONSIDER

Following are a number of situations that pose problems related to the subject of this chapter. There are no right or wrong "answers" to these situations. They are presented simply to stimulate your thinking about retirement and to emphasize certain aspects of retirement planning. It is not necessary to arrive at any particular conclusion about each case.

It's a good idea for couples to review the situations separately and then share their thoughts. If you are single, perhaps you have a friend, relative, or clergyman with whom you can exchange ideas. Discussing situations like these can help to clarify key aspects of retirement planning and will enable you to become more in tune with your feelings and those of others.

Situation 1: First Things First

Ed and Dotti are both fifty-five years old and expect to retire in ten years. They are trying to think through which areas in retirement are most important to plan for now and which can wait until later. How soon before retirement should they be planning for the following things?

_____Whether or not to move when they retire
_____How big a home to have
_____Where retirement income will come from
_____How to budget retirement income
_____Having a will

_____What to do in retirement
_____Getting a part-time job
_____How much health insurance to have in retirement and what kind
_____Living alone

Thoughts to Consider

1. Which of these concerns could have harmful consequences if there were little or no planning for them?
2. Which ones do people tend to put off until the last minute? Why?
3. Are there concerns other than these that require planning? What are they?
4. Try ranking the list above according to your personal priorities.

Situation 2: Feelings About Retirement

Mike has mixed feelings about his pending retirement. On some days he talks excitedly about never having to work again. But on other days he is a little anxious and concerned. What are some things that might account for Mike's different feelings?

Thoughts to Consider

1. How do you think most people feel about retirement? Is Mike's case typical?
2. Do people often put on a good show of having no worries about retirement when they really are confused or anxious? Why?
3. How can we overcome our fears, apprehensions, or anxieties about retirement?

Situation 3: "The Masculine Role"

Theresa and Harold both work. He, with a sigh of relief, will retire next month, and she in two years. She could take early retirement when he retires, but she hesitates. She likes her job. When they discuss it, they usually end up arguing. He thinks she should retire when he does—says he's not retiring to be alone and to do the housework. What do you think?

Possible Approaches

1. It's a wife's obligation to retire when her husband does.
2. They are two separate people and are entitled to make separate decisions.
3. Harold should find something to keep him busy over the next two years.
4. They should compromise on Theresa working one more year.

Thoughts to Consider

1. Why does Harold want Theresa to retire when he does?
2. If Harold retires and Theresa doesn't, how should the household duties be handled and by whom?
3. Harold is scheduled to retire next month, so why haven't they settled this issue by now?

B.C.   by johnny hart

Situation 4: Where to Begin?

George is a good planner. He keeps things moving. He likes his job and, to his wife Marion's dismay, frequently takes his work home. Marion is concerned that he is not doing enough planning for their retirement ten years from now. He says it's too early and shows some irritation when she presses the matter. Who should start where, and when?

Possible Approaches

1. She should start planning their future by herself.
2. He's right, it is too early—wait a few years.
3. Forget it! Life is too unpredictable anyway.

Thoughts to Consider

1. Do you think this is a fairly common situation?
2. Can Marion just go ahead and begin planning by herself?
   (a) What things can she begin working on?
   (b) What things do they need to plan together?
3. Is there an outside source to help George and Marion come to a common understanding?
4. Is retirement planning worth arguing and bickering over?

Situation 5: The Values of School

Harriet is fifty and plans to work for years to come. But she also wants to go back to school at night to take some courses. Her husband Roger is discouraging her. School is for young people, he says, and the time needed for study would take away from time they now have together. What should Harriet do?

Thoughts to Consider

1. Do you think there are advantages in Harriet returning to school? Disadvantages?
2. If you had the chance to go back to school, what kinds of courses would you take?
3. What are the skills of a good student no matter what age?

REFERENCES AND RESOURCES

Arthur, Julietta K. *Retire to Action—A Guide to Voluntary Service.* Nashville, Tenn.: Abingdon Press.

Comfort, Alex. *A Good Age.* New York: Simon & Schuster, 1976.

Consumer Information Catalog. Published four times each year by the federal government. It lists booklets from almost thirty government agencies on such topics as automobiles, health and health care, employment and education, and housing. To get on the catalog mailing list, write to the Consumer Information Center, Pueblo, CO 81009.

Consumer's Resource Handbook. Published by the White House Office of the Special Assistant for Consumer Affairs. Single copies may be obtained by writing the Consumer Information Center, Dept. 532G, Pueblo, CO 81009.

De Beauvoir, Simone. *Coming of Age.* New York: G.P. Putnam & Sons, 1972.

Disston, Harry. *Beginning the Rest of Your Life: A Guide to an Active Retirement.* New York: Crown Publishers (Arlington House), 1981.

Elliott, Gordon, and Mary Elliott. *The Ideal Life: 50 and Over.* Milwaukee, Wis.: Ideals (11315 Watertown Plank Road 53226), 1980.

Frost, Marie. *Making the Most of Your Golden Years.* Cincinnati: Standard Publishing Co., 1982.

Galton, Lawrence. *Don't Give Up On an Aging Parent.* New York: Crown Publishers, 1975.

Garrison, Ronald B., and Clark M. England. *Retirement: A Time for Fulfillment,* revised ed. Logan, Utah: Center for Professional Development, 1982.

Hunter, Woodrow W. *Preparation for Retirement.* Ann Arbor, Mich.: Institute of Gerontology, University of Michigan, and Wayne State University, 1973.

Knopf, Olga, M.D. *Successful Aging.* New York: The Viking Press, 1975.

Nelson, Pearl A. *The First Year: Retirement Journal.* Buffalo, N.Y.: Potentials Development, Inc. (775 Main St., Suite 321, 14203), 1982.

Oberleder, Muriel. *The Aging Trap: How to Get Over Being Young,* Washington, D.C.: Acropolis Books, 1982.

Osgood, Nancy J. *Life After Work: Retirement, Leisure, Recreation and the Elderly.* New York: Praeger Publishers, 1982.

Otte, Elmer. *Retirement Rehearsal Guidebook.* Appleton, Wisc.: Retirement Research (Box 401, 54912), 1980.

Portfolio of Vital Information. Available free from the National Retired Teachers Association, 1909 K St., N.W., Washington, DC 20006. Highly recommended.

Selected U.S. Government Publications. A pamphlet published by the federal government listing booklets on a wide variety of topics. To get on the mailing list for this catalog, write to the Superintendent of Documents, Washington, DC 20402.

Silverstone, Barbara, and Helen Kandel Hyman. *You and Your Aging Parent.* New York: Pantheon Books, 1976.

Smaridge, Norah. *Choosing Your Retirement Hobby.* New York: Dodd, Mead, 1976.

U.S. Department of HHS, Office of Human Development, Administration on Aging. This agency prints a booklet containing a list of publications on such topics as retirement planning, employment opportunities, consumer guides, and legal matters. Available from the Superintendent of Documents, U.S. Government Printing Office, Washington, DC 20402.

Your Retirement Psychology Guide and *Your Retirement Hobby Guide.* Washington, D.C.: American Association of Retired Persons (1909 K St., N.W., 20006).

Chapter 2
Health and Well-Being

CHAPTER 2 WARM-UP

Before reading "Health and Well-Being," test your general knowledge of the subject by placing a check mark next to the answer you prefer. Check the key at the end to find the correct answer.

1. Older adults shouldn't start an exercise program.   True_____ False_____

2. Generic drugs are chemically the same as brand-name drugs.   True_____ False_____

3. Most forms of cancer are curable if discovered early.   True_____ False_____

4. Whether you drink or not is really none of your doctor's business.   True_____ False_____

5. If you smoke for a number of years, then quit, the damage is done and nothing will reverse it.   True_____ False_____

6. Being overweight can shorten your life.   True_____ False_____

7. An individual has little control over his or her health.   True_____ False_____

8. No single food contains all the nutrients we need.   True_____ False_____

9. Medicare will not cover all costs of an illness or injury.   True_____ False_____

10. For many people, home health care is a valuable alternative to hospitalization or institutionalization.   True_____ False_____

Key: 1. (F), 2. (T), 3. (T), 4. (F), 5. (F), 6. (T), 7. (F), 8. (T), 9. (T), 10. (T).

HEALTH MAINTENANCE—AN ATTITUDE

When you think about retirement, one of the areas you probably will be very concerned with is your health. While most of us value our health highly, we often take it for granted until illness occurs. When health is lost, it is missed dearly. Indeed, illness and disability are often felt as profoundly disturbing and fearful experiences. Not only does illness prevent us from engaging in many activities, but it may also make us overdependent on others and drain us of both emotional and financial resources.

Is health simply a matter of luck? Is it inherited from our ancestors? Does an individual have any control over health at all? Most health care professionals say that individual behavior is a major factor in determining a person's overall health. This chapter is mostly concerned with what we as individuals can do to stay healthy, to regain health if illness strikes, or to cope with a long-term illness. We will also discuss some of the major health problems experienced by many as they grow older. The last part of the chapter takes a look at the business end of health care: choosing a physician, paying for medical care, and understanding the various types of health-care services available in the community.

Before we begin, it may be worthwhile to ask a deceptively simple question: "What is health?"

Health is not just the absence of disease, but is a state of complete physical, mental, social, and spiritual well-being. These four factors work together to determine our total state of health. In this sense total health is an ideal, or a goal for us to strive for. Our state of health, then, is judged not only by the condition of our various body parts, but also by other factors that may be equally important.

AGING IS NOT A DISEASE

It is important to recognize that normal aging does not represent a disease process. Our bodies undergo normal biological changes as we grow older that may result in reduced performance and greater vulnerability to disease. But the aging of our bodies and of particular organs is not a disease itself.

What are some of the changes that take place as we age? Let's look at them by dividing them into two areas: changes that are physical and changes that are emotional. All along, however, we need to keep in mind how changes in one area can bring about changes in the other.

Physical Changes

Among the changes that may be experienced as we grow older are drying of the skin, reduced muscle size, increased brittleness of bones, decreased vision and color perception, reduced hearing ability, especially in the high-frequency tones, less acute senses of taste and smell, reduced heart and lung capacity, and decreased kidney function.

Of course, all of these changes do not necessarily happen to the same person or over the same time span. Physical changes come at different times for different people. For this reason, we cannot draw up stereotypes of what people at age sixty-five or eighty should be like. There are eighty-year-olds who can still play a good game of tennis, and forty-year-olds who are so out of shape that a good game could put a severe strain on their heart. There are fifty-year-olds who have lost interest in sex, and seventy-five-year-olds for whom sex is a regular and wonderful part of their life. The opposites, of course, are also true.

Even though we can detect certain tendencies that occur with aging, they should not lead us to believe that each person's case will be similar. We age individually. Nor should we confuse supposed signs of aging with what may be more directly the result of poor diet, lack of exercise, or other factors that we have some control over. Changes in body function are normal and to be expected, but symptoms of confusion and/or pain are abnormal and should be considered warning signs of possible health problems.

Emotional Changes

Besides physical changes, there are also emotional changes that we undergo as we age. Certainly, here too the stereotypes of the personalities of "older people" need to be challenged. The pictures of a silly, doting old fool, of a dirty old man, or of a senile eccentric are not typical of people who reach a certain age. A silly old fool was, no doubt, a silly young fool; a dirty old man, a dirty young man; and an eccentric, one all his or her life. People don't undergo great emotional changes just because they reach a certain age. Basic personality traits are likely to continue throughout one's life. New ones that develop usually do so over long periods of time or are brought on by crisis situations or physical illnesses.

In many ways society's images of people who are "old" and the social patterns of discrimination against "older people" can have powerful emotional consequences on people. They can bring about feelings of uselessness and lead to depression.

Depression is one of the most common emotional problems found in persons over sixty. Some indicators of the presence of depression are feelings of helplessness, sadness, lack of vitality, frequent feelings of guilt, loneliness, boredom, sexual disinterest, impotence, and insomnia.

One great factor that can contribute to depression is the death of someone near to us. In our middle years we are not likely to lose many people except for parents and a few others. But when we are in our sixties or older, we will likely experience the loss of a number of close friends and relatives in our age group—sisters, brothers, friends, fellow workers. It is no easy matter to deal with so many losses. Certainly, it will affect us very deeply.

PREVENTION

As we mentioned earlier, health is determined by a number of factors working together. There is no doubt, however, that physical health is a big factor in overall health. And health experts agree that there is a great deal that we as individuals can do to maintain and improve our physical health. The key steps toward prevention of disease and illness are:

- Maintaining a balance of physical activity and rest.
- Maintaining an adequate diet.
- Weight control.
- Avoiding excess use of substances known to be harmful.

- Maintaining a healthy emotional outlook.
- Minimizing and controlling stress.

Let's take a closer look at each of these.

The Value of Exercise

A regular exercise program helps the body adapt to reduced circulation brought on by arteriosclerosis, increases the oxygen-carrying capacity of the blood, improves the bellows action of the chest, enhances liver and kidney function, improves muscle tone, stimulates mineralization of the bones, and reduces fat deposits. Regular exercise can also improve your ability to relax, to control emotional tension, and to combat fatigue. Exercise is also an excellent way to help control your weight.

Exercise has been proven to promote the growth of additional blood vessels that take over the role of narrowing main coronary vessels feeding the heart muscle. This is particularly important for men in the preretirement age category, many of whom may be in the early to middle stages of the development of heart disease. For such people, exercise can indeed be lifesaving.

There are other values to regular exercise aside from those mentioned above, especially if it is done outdoors: the pleasure of breathing fresh air, of smelling scents in the wind, of observing the beauties of nature and feeling alive. There is no way to measure these benefits to the spirit.

What kind of exercise is best? Exercise can take a wide variety of forms, depending on your interests and abilities. It is important to know some safety rules, however, including the necessity of having a thorough medical checkup before beginning a major new exercise routine. Your physician will examine you for evidence of heart or lung disease and will advise you as to the safety of various kinds of exercise for your physical condition.

Fitness experts declare that the best kinds of exercise are those that put a steady load on your heart/lung system. While there is value in exercises that involve work-pause routines (such as tennis or gardening), the most beneficial are those rhythmic exercises that put prolonged, but not too severe, strain on the heart, followed by periods of semi-rest. Such exercises include dancing, rope skipping, skating, jogging, bicycle riding, swimming, cross-country skiing, rowing, and hiking. Walking is also an excellent and popular form of exercise provided it is done at a fairly brisk pace and for a long enough period of time.

These forms of exercise are the most beneficial, but only if they are done on a regular and continuing basis. Doctors recommend that an exercise program be followed at least three days per week. And care should be taken not to try a full routine right at the beginning. When the jogging fad began several years ago, a large number of heart attacks and bone and muscle injuries were reported because too many people failed to build endurance gradually.

In addition to maintaining or improving your present health and increasing your chances of enjoying a healthy retirement, a regular exercise program has another benefit. Exercise improves our sense of well-being and brightens our psychological state. There is also evidence of increased worker productivity among those engaged in a regular physical exercise program.

Rest

While it may be obvious that rest and sleep are needed by everyone, many find it difficult to relax and to get a restful night of sleep. Some may have trouble sleeping due to nervousness or physical discomfort stemming from problems such as arthritis or skin irritations. It's difficult to maintain good health and spirits without sleeping well at night. In cases of recurring sleep problems, a physician should be consulted.

There are a number of other ways to rest and relax, and many people have their favorite techniques. These might include a hot bath, a before- or after-dinner cocktail or glass of wine, or yoga. Most yoga practitioners in the United States do not do so for spiritual purposes, but only as an exercise to achieve greater relaxation of the body and mind, or to promote muscle flexibility.

Adequate Nutrition

No single food contains all the nutrients we need. Nutritionists tell us that an adequate diet consisting of the proper amounts from the four basic food groups will provide us with the many known nutrients needed by the body.

The basic food groups are meats, fruits and vegetables, breads and cereals, and milk and milk products. The daily food guide on page 60 shows that the average adult can meet the recommended dietary allowance by consuming daily two servings from the milk group, five ounces from the meat group, four servings from the bread–cereal group, and four servings from the vegetable–fruit group.

What about vitamin supplements? Vitamins are a multimillion dollar industry in our country today. Most experts agree, however, that if you eat a balanced diet containing the proper amounts of each of the four basic food groups, you probably don't need to supplement with vitamin pills.

Weight Control

Many of the leading health problems in our country today are related to overeating and excess weight. Such problems include heart and other circulatory diseases, stress on joints, greater tendency to diabetes, high blood pressure, and aggravation of arthritis.

Not only is it important to monitor how much we eat, but we should watch the kinds of food we take in as well. Fats and oils, for example, contain over twice the number of calories per unit of weight as carbohydrates and proteins. In addition, there is abundant evidence that people with diets containing greater amounts of animal fats are significantly more likely to develop heart and circulatory diseases.

Perhaps a few words about diets are in order. There are a number of fad diets in use today, many of which are of little value: the egg diet, the grapefruit diet, the water diet, the martini diet, the high protein diet, and a host of others. Each promises what the others don't deliver: permanent and healthy weight loss. Some of these diets can be downright dangerous.

The simple formula for true weight loss is as follows: Take in fewer calories than you expend, and you will lose weight. If you take in more calories than you expend, you will gain weight. Crash diets are almost never advisable. Nutritionists agree that rarely is weight loss of more than two pounds per week advisable. For many, the key to effective dieting is in changing eating habits. If nervousness or boredom is at the root of a big appetite, doing something about these feelings may do much to help a dieter be successful. Sometimes dieting is easier when combined with a regular exercise program because more calories are used up in exercise. Thus the need to cut down on food intake becomes less. For more detailed information on wise dieting, see your physician, your local cooperative extension office, or a local self-help group.

Harmful Substances

Studies on alcohol and tobacco use show clearly that excessive use of these substances will almost invariably result in serious health problems.

Studies show that heavy smokers are much more likely to be victims of heart disease than nonsmokers. Death rates from heart attacks in men range from 50 to 200 percent higher among smokers than among nonsmokers. In addition to contributing to and aggravating heart disease, cigarette smoking is linked to a number of other serious medical problems such as emphysema, cancer, pneumonia, influenza, and others.

Studies also show that the danger of experiencing one or more of these health problems is directly related to the amount smoked. On the brighter side, it has been shown that the chances of smoking adversely affecting your health are reduced a good deal if you quit, even after smoking for a number of years.

If you smoke, you may want to take a good hard look at the possible consequences for yourself as well as for those close to you. And at today's prices a pack-a-day smoker would save several hundred dollars each year by not smoking.

It has long been recognized in our society that excessive use of alcohol is a major problem. It was always assumed, however, that among the elderly it was

THE WIZARD OF ID   by Brant parker and Johnny hart

not really too serious an issue. We are slowly coming to realize that alcohol plays an important role in many of the health and social problems experienced by older people.

Beer, wine, and whiskey, while low in fat and cholesterol, are high in calories and have little if any nutritional value. While some studies have shown that small quantities of alcohol can be beneficial by reducing stress, detrimental effects of more than moderate alcohol consumption on the health of millions of Americans have reached epidemic proportions. Added to this is the incredibly high percentage of auto accidents that involve a driver who has been drinking.

What Are the Signs of Alcoholism?*

1. YES NO Do you occasionally drink heavily after a disappointment, a quarrel, or when the boss gives you a hard time?
2. YES NO When you have trouble or feel under pressure, do you always drink more heavily than usual?
3. YES NO Have you noticed that you are able to handle more liquor than you did when you were first drinking?
4. YES NO Did you ever wake up on the "morning after" and find that you could not remember part of the past evening, even though your friends say you did not "pass out?"
5. YES NO When drinking with other people, do you try to have a few extra drinks when others will not know it?
6. YES NO Are there certain occasions when you feel uncomfortable if alcohol is not available?
7. YES NO Have you recently noticed that when you begin drinking you are in more of a hurry to get the first drink than you used to be?
8. YES NO Do you sometimes feel a little guilty about your drinking?
9. YES NO Are you secretly irritated when your family or friends discuss your drinking?
10. YES NO Have you recently noticed an increase in frequency of your memory blackouts?
11. YES NO Do you often find that you wish to continue drinking after friends say they have had enough?
12. YES NO Do you usually have a reason for the occasions when you drink heavily?
13. YES NO When sober, do you often regret things you have done or said while drinking?
14. YES NO Have you tried switching brands or following various plans to control your drinking?
15. YES NO Have you often failed to keep the promise you have made to yourself about controlling or cutting down on your drinking?
16. YES NO Have you ever tried to control your drinking by changing jobs or moving?
17. YES NO Do you try to avoid family or close friends while you are drinking?

---

*Reprinted by permission of the National Council on Alcoholism, Inc.

18. YES NO Are you having an increasing number of financial and work problems?
19. YES NO Do more people seem to be treating you unfairly without good reason?
20. YES NO Do you eat very little or irregularly when you are drinking?
21. YES NO Do you sometimes have the "shakes" in the morning and find that it helps to have a little drink?
22. YES NO Have you recently noticed that you cannot drink as much as you once did?
23. YES NO Do you sometimes stay drunk for several days at a time?
24. YES NO Do you sometimes feel very depressed and wonder whether life is worth living?
25. YES NO Sometimes, after periods of drinking, do you see or hear things that aren't there?
26. YES NO Do you get terribly frightened after you have been drinking heavily?

A "yes" to *any* of the questions indicates possible symptoms of alcoholism. "Yes" answers to several questions indicate various stages of alcoholism. Several "yes" answers to the questions in group 1–8 may indicate an early stage; several "yes" answers to the questions in group 9–21 may indicate the middle stage; several "yes" answers to the questions in group 22–26 indicate a later stage.

If you or someone you know has a problem with alcohol, help is available. Call the local number listed in your telephone directory for Alcoholics Anonymous (for problem drinkers) or Al-Anon (for family members). People who understand the disease of alcoholism through personal experience are available to help you, day or night.

It is extremely dangerous to combine alcohol with certain prescribed medications. An estimated 2,500 deaths a year, most of them unintentional, occur in the United States because of drug–alcohol interactions. If you drink even moderate amounts of alcohol, and that includes beer, wine, or hard liquor, ask your physician if you can continue to do so safely when taking a prescribed medication.

There is some evidence that excessive consumption of caffeine has a detrimental effect on the heart. Although this effect has not been proven beyond doubt, the safest course is probably to avoid consuming large amounts of beverages containing caffeine, such as regular coffee, tea, and many soft drinks.

Thus far, we have been primarily discussing steps the individual can take to help assure that good health is maintained. We said that regular exercise, adequate rest and relaxation, a proper diet, weight control, avoiding overuse of certain harmful substances, and having a healthy mental outlook are all key ingredients in positive health. But despite our efforts, sometimes illness does present itself. Contributing factors may be environmental hazards, heredity, advancing age, or simply our own choice of behavior.

In some cases we may not be aware that we have a disease. This can happen, for example, with high blood pressure (HBP). It is estimated that sixty million Americans may have HBP, persistently high arterial blood pressure. Because this disease is so common, everyone should have a blood pressure test once a year.

Most cases of high blood pressure cannot be cured, but can be controlled by continuous treatment. It appears that a person is more likely to have HBP if

someone else in their family has or had it. You can develop HBP even if you are usually a calm, relaxed person. Some risk factors associated with HBP are obesity and diets high in salt content.

If your doctor determines you have mild HBP he may recommend that you lose weight, eat less salt, or get more exercise. But if you need medication to reduce your blood pressure you will most likely need to watch your weight and diet, and continue taking medication for the rest of your life.

High blood pressure can lead to many serious conditions in older adults including stroke, heart disease, and kidney failure. So watching your blood pressure and taking the necessary steps to control it can be vital to your long-term good health.

Early detection of any form of disease is the prime reason why regular physical checkups are so important for middle-aged and older adults. Whenever possible, try to participate in health screening programs offered through various groups in your community.

When a health problem comes to our attention we are faced with decisions that, to a large extent, will determine the course of the illness. In the following paragraphs we will discuss some of these decisions and what can be done to help regain health if illness should strike.

Coping with Stress

Here are some suggestions middle-aged and older people have given for dealing with stress:

1. Make plans. Knowing what you plan to do in the future helps reduce the stress of uncertainty.
2. Don't try to do too much in too little time. Learn your limitations and stay within them.
3. Conserve your energy.
4. Develop a network of friends you can count on in times of trouble. This should include at least one friend with whom you can share everything about your life.
5. Maintain the positive feelings of hope and self-confidence.
6. Anticipate future stresses.

Years ago, very little connection was made between physical health and emotional well-being. Today, however, there is a great deal of evidence showing that our state of mind is a key factor in staying healthy and in recovering from illness. This also means that our ability to handle stress is directly related to our ability to stay physically healthy. It is well known, for example, that those who work in stressful situations are more prone to stomach ulcers.

Handling stress is extremely important to those entering retirement. Despite the common belief that retirement means finally quitting the rat race, studies show that, for many, the first months and years of retirement are an extremely stressful time. Our social relationships may be disrupted, income may be reduced rather drastically, and feelings of self-worth may decline.

For someone who is down in the dumps after retirement, well-meaning advice to "look on the brighter side" probably does little to alleviate feelings of boredom and uselessness. While adjusting to retirement is discussed more fully in another chapter, it is important to note here that one's physical health can be powerfully affected by such feelings. A person who is depressed and unhappy is a prime target for a serious illness or accident. And even if illness doesn't strike, the individual is missing out on the real value of good health: being able to engage in those activities that bring personal satisfaction and that make life enjoyable.

ILLNESS—TIME FOR DECISIONS

Early in this chapter we recognized the fearful experience that illness can be. The threat posed by a disease is real and disturbing. There is a natural tendency, therefore, to want the signs and symptoms of the illness to just go away. Unfortunately, wishing this rarely makes it so. The result is that many people just refuse to recognize the signs when they appear. This may or may not be a conscious decision but the hope is that, if evidence of illness is ignored, maybe it will eventually somehow disappear.

Sometimes it takes a good deal of courage to admit to ourselves that we are sick or that we might have a symptom of a potentially serious illness. There is danger, however, in deluding ourselves by thinking we are not ill or in self-diagnosing a problem as being merely temporary and unimportant. The classic example of this for women is a lump or thickening in the breast. Many women do not regularly perform breast self-exams for fear of finding a lump that could mean breast cancer. And even some of those who do discover a lump or thickening in the breast delay seeing their physician in hopes that it will go away of its own accord. Tragically for many, by the time action is taken, it is too late, and radical surgery becomes necessary.

This example is a drastic one, but there are a number of similar situations, some not so serious, some just as serious, in which people must decide whether or not to seek medical attention. Unfortunately, in many cases over-the-counter remedies are sought that treat the signs and symptoms of the problem but fail to get at the cause. Such action can be dangerous by hiding the seriousness of the problem until it worsens to the point where the over-the-counter remedy is no longer effective. By this time, even appropriate medical attention may not be sufficient to prevent serious and long-term consequences.

The earlier a health problem is detected and treated, the greater the chances are of complete recovery, or of keeping harmful effects to a minimum.

The best advice, then, is to consult your physician if there are persistent signs or symptoms of a health problem.

Equally important is following carefully the advice and instructions of your physician in regard to medication, rest, and activity. Many drug therapies, for example, are effective only if taken in the proper dosages and for appropriate time periods. Similarly, the effectiveness of some drugs is negated if combined with certain foods or liquids or taken immediately prior to or following meals. Be sure to ask your physician or pharmacist about any such special requirements of a medication you are prescribed.

There are many times when physicians disagree on the best course of action with a particular illness. For this reason, if a physician recommends that you undergo a surgical procedure, it's a good idea to seek a second opinion from another physician. This practice is becoming much more widespread, and some health insurance policies will pay for the visit to another physician for the second opinion.

Clearly, *you* play a key role in recovering from illness. By facing up to the possibility of illness, by seeking appropriate medical care, and by carefully following the advice of health professionals, you can significantly increase the probability of a satisfactory outcome.

Adjusting to Chronic Illness

Usually, we think of prevention as action taken to avoid illness and disability. But it can also mean something else. If we become a victim of a chronic illness, such as diabetes, arthritis, or heart disease, there are steps we can take to prevent the condition from having a disastrous effect on other aspects of life.

Chronic illness sometimes brings with it pain, increased dependency on others, disrupted family relations, financial burden, and despondency. Those who have become incapacitated may feel that they have become a great burden on their spouse or family. They may also become worried and fearful about being abandoned, or feel terribly down about being so helpless. At such times, counseling services provided by disease- or disability-related associations, such as the local chapter of the Arthritis Foundation, may be extremely helpful.

Private, nonprofit organizations, such as the American Lung Association, the American Heart Association, and others can also be very helpful in providing educational services, equipment, transportation, and arrangements for rehabilitation services.

THE WIZARD OF ID   by Brant parker and Johnny hart

Those who have chronic illness can help themselves by following their doctor's instructions, and by utilizing the resources available through organizations such as those mentioned above as well as through local departments of public health.

Chronic illness also has an effect on those who are close to an ill person. At the beginning of the illness, they may have been extremely helpful and able to show deep understanding and patience. In time, however, the situation may become very wearing on them. They may feel cheated over having to make so many sacrifices. They may become irritated and even angry at times, then feel guilty for their seeming selfishness. It's a difficult problem and very hard to deal with. Such feelings are natural and expected, however, and it does not mean that the person is callous or uncaring. Everyone at times needs a break from such continuous responsibilities.

Frequent short periods of relief and open communication can do much to help out in such situations. Having someone to talk to about the situation, such as a member of the clergy or another professional helper, can also be helpful. Or there may be opportunities to be part of a discussion or mutual support group in which persons who are facing the same problem talk about how they are dealing with it.

MAJOR HEALTH PROBLEMS

Heart Disease

More than half of all people who die each year in the United States are victims of diseases of the heart and circulatory system. The most common such disease, arteriosclerosis, or hardening of the arteries, is a process that occurs over a period of many years. The buildup of fatty deposits within the arteries gradually clogs them, blocking the flow of oxygen-rich blood. This puts a tremendous strain on the heart. When the buildup occurs in arteries feeding the heart muscle itself (coronary arteries), the result may be angina, or heart pain, resulting from too little oxygen-carrying blood reaching an area of the heart. If the artery becomes completely blocked, the result is a heart attack, wherein some of the tissues of the heart actually die from lack of oxygen and scar tissue is formed.

As mentioned earlier in the chapter, studies show that there is a strong relationship between lifelong eating habits and the development of heart

THE WIZARD OF ID   by Brant parker and Johnny hart

disease. Those whose diets contain high levels of saturated fats are significantly more likely to develop heart disease than are those who consume moderate or small amounts. Saturated fats are found primarily in beef and pork, shellfish, and organ meats. Middle-aged men who are 20 percent or more overweight are about three times as likely to have a fatal heart attack as middle-aged men of normal weight.

Stroke

Stroke is damage to the brain caused by either a hemorrhage or a blood clot. A hemorrhage is the rupture of a weakened artery in the brain. When a rupture occurs some brain cells are no longer receiving the oxygen-rich blood they need. Similarly, the formation of a clot in the brain cuts off the oxygen supply to nearby cells. In both cases, the result can be minor or severe paralysis, loss of memory, difficulty in speaking, and impaired vision. A stroke does not normally cause pain. The indication that something is wrong is that some part of the body fails to function. If you have such an experience, or witness one, a doctor should be notified immediately.

Cancer

THE SEVEN EARLY DANGER SIGNALS OF CANCER*

1. Unusual bleeding or discharge.
2. A lump or thickening in the breast or elsewhere.
3. A sore that does not heal.
4. Change in bowel or bladder habits.
5. Hoarseness or cough.
6. Indigestion or difficulty in swallowing.
7. Change in a wart or mole.

*Courtesy American Cancer Society.

The second leading cause of death among Americans is cancer. Although this disease is not part of the aging process itself, it is much more common in older individuals. While there is still much to learn about cancer, recent research has greatly increased knowledge about prevention and treatment.

The greatest weapon available against cancer is early detection. The five-year survival rate for almost all kinds of cancer is far greater if the disease is discovered in its early stages rather than after it has had a chance to spread to nearby regions of the body. In the case of bladder cancer, for example, 72 percent of those in whom it is discovered early are alive five years later, whereas only 21 percent of those in whom it is not discovered early are alive after five years.

You can combat cancer by following these three important steps:

1. Learn the warning signals of cancer.
2. See your physician immediately if you notice any of these danger signals.
3. Have periodic medical examinations.

In addition, the American Cancer Society recommends the actions shown below as protection against various types of cancer:

SAFEGUARDS URGED BY THE AMERICAN CANCER SOCIETY*

Lungs: Reduce and ultimately eliminate cigarette smoking.

Colon &
Rectum: Induce a proctoscopic exam in physical checkups if over age 50 every three to five years after two initial negative sigmoidoscopies one year apart.

Breast: Perform breast self-exams as a monthly female practice.

Uterus: Have a pap test at least yearly.

Skin: Avoid excessive exposure to the sun.

Oral: Visit your dentist or dental hygienist regularly for exams.

Basic: Have regular physical examinations.

* Courtesy American Cancer Society.

Arthritis

Arthritis is an umbrella term used for up to a hundred different types of rheumatic disease. Common symptoms of the disease are pain, stiffness, and usually inflammation in one or more joints. There are no cures for arthritis, but seeking treatment from a qualified physician or clinic is the first, all-important step toward living successfully with the disease.

Success of an arthritis treatment program depends largely on how faithfully it is carried out by the patient. The earlier proper treatment is started, the better the chances are of escaping pain and disability. Typical arthritis warning signs are:

1. Persistent pain and stiffness on rising.
2. Pain, tenderness, or swelling in one or more joints.
3. Recurrence of these symptoms, especially when they involve more than one joint.
4. Recurrence of persistent pain and stiffness in the neck, lower back, knees, and other joints.

If you should experience any of these symptoms, a physician should be consulted. You will probably be asked to rest and relax more than is your custom, to avoid fatigue and worry. Exercises may also be prescribed. A nourishing diet may also be recommended to help maintain proper weight or to shed extra pounds that may aggravate the arthritis by placing unnecessary strain on joints.

There are a number of misconceptions regarding arthritis. Many believe that a warm climate will prevent or correct arthritis. While there is no evidence that the disease itself changes or gets better in a warm, dry climate, some people report greater comfort in such areas. Others, however, find no change at all.

Many people also believe that special diets or exotic foods are helpful. There is no evidence that any nutritional deficiency causes arthritis, or that any food or vitamin is effective in treating or curing it.

Unfortunately, many people with arthritis do not follow treatment procedures. High-powered advertising for products to relieve arthritis often is misleading and tempts people to bypass the doctor and seek quick answers to their problems. Such ads also give the impression that arthritis is mostly a disease of minor aches and pains. Products and treatments offered by such ads may not be harmful, but they waste money and are dangerous if used as a substitute for qualified care.

Diabetes

Diabetes is a disease of carbohydrate metabolism; the body does not make proper use of certain foods. Thought to be hereditary, diabetes is caused either by too little insulin or by a defect in the action of insulin, which is a hormone produced by the pancreas. Diabetes is characterized by polyuria and excessive amounts of sugar in the blood and urine.

Various terms are used to identify the kinds of diabetes. Early-onset diabetes is often a severe form, usually acquired during youth. Mature-onset diabetes many times is a milder form that frequently develops in overweight individuals in middle age or later.

The onset of diabetes is marked by frequent urination, extreme thirst, and constant hunger. Other symptoms include tiring easily, weight loss, slow-healing infections, and itching.

There is no total cure for diabetes. The condition can be controlled, however, with proper care. Not all diabetics require medication. All diabetics must control their diet and activity. Many cases of diabetes can be treated with weight loss and proper diet and exercise habits.

ORAL HEALTH

Oral hygiene is a matter of concern for most people for reasons of personal appearance. It is also important because it may have a strong influence on nutrition, which is vital at all ages. Unfortunately, oral health is an area that many people neglect, resulting in periodontal disease—an inflammatory disease of the tissues surrounding and supporting the teeth and a leading cause of tooth loss.

Periodontal disease is a slow and cumulative process that begins early in life as a direct result of poor oral hygiene. Actual tooth loss may begin in early middle age. And the disease is very common. In the forty-five to sixty-four age group more than three fourths of all people with any natural teeth have periodontal disease; above the age of sixty-five, the percentage is even higher.

The keys to preventing or arresting the progress of periodontal disease are home care and professional attention. Regular and frequent brushing and flossing are extremely important. For those who have difficulty brushing or flossing, an electric toothbrush and a water irrigator may be very helpful.

Those who have either a partial or full denture should make sure it fits properly. Dentures should be soaked each night and brushed regularly with a denture brush.

Another important oral health measure is to have mouth tissues examined regularly for signs of oral cancer. Evidence such as an irritated area that doesn't heal or any other unusual sign should be brought to your dentist's attention promptly.

THE WIZARD OF ID   **by Brant parker and Johnny hart**

Even if there are no signs or symptoms of disease of any kind, it's wise to have periodic checkups in order to maintain good oral health.

MEDICARE

Medicare is a federal health insurance program for people sixty-five or older and certain disabled people. The Medicare program has two parts, hospital insurance and medical insurance. The hospital insurance (known as Part A), helps pay for inpatient hospital care, inpatient care in a skilled nursing facility under certain conditions, and home health care. There is no insurance premium for this hospital insurance but the individual must pay an annual deductible and a portion of the hospital care, according to current guidelines.

The medical insurance part of Medicare (known as Part B) helps pay for "medically necessary" doctor's services, outpatient hospital services, and certain other medical items and services not covered by hospital insurance. It can also help pay for home health services. The cost of this optional medical insurance is shared by the individual and the federal government. Those who choose to buy the medical insurance pay their share through automatic deductions from their Social Security check. This premium rises each year according to the Social Security cost of living adjustment. The individual must also pay a deductible and 20 percent of the amount approved by Medicare for the particular medical services provided.

Payments for medical services under Part B of Medicare often cover only a portion of your physician's bill. Medicare will pay only what are defined as "reasonable charges"—which are determined by your local Medicare insurance carrier. Because of the way approved amounts are determined and because of high rates of inflation in health care, the charges approved are often less than the actual cost. Medicare insurance pays 80 percent of the approved charge, even if it is less than the actual charge.

Medicare Assignment

Medicare has predetermined amounts it will pay for various medical procedures and services. If a doctor agrees to accept the amount Medicare approves as full payment then he or she is said to be "accepting assignment." In such a case the physician bills Medicare directly and you pay only the annual deductible and the remaining 20 percent not covered by Medicare.

If you need help or advice on Medicare benefits, contact your local Social Security office.

How To Get Faster Medicare Claim Processing

There are a number of guidelines to follow to ensure that claims under Medicare's medical insurance are processed as quickly as possible. Most of these tips are covered in a leaflet called, "How To Complete the Patient's Request for Medicare Payment," available at any Social Security office.

The most common mistakes that result in delays are made in completing the Patient's Request for Medicare Payment form—Form 1490S. Missing information or not enough information on a claim can cause delays. The mishaps may include:

- Failure to sign the claim form.
- Failure to include the claim number. It should be copied from the Medicare card (include the letter at the end of the number).
- Failure to send to the correct address. There's a list of organizations in the booklet "Your Medicare Handbook" that shows which one services Medicare medical insurance claims for particular geographical areas.
- Failure to itemize bills. Each bill submitted must show the date and place the services or supplies were received, the description of each service, the charge for each service or supply, and the doctor's or supplier's name.

Don't "bunch" or hold on to bills in hopes of reducing paperwork or expediting payment by sending them all at one time. This increases the chances of making a mistake and increases the possibility of affecting the flow of Medicare claims, which could affect the speed with which his or her claims are processed. As soon as covered bills come to the current deductible, they should be sent in. Then future bills should be sent as they are received so that Medicare can pay them promptly.

WHEN MEDICARE IS NOT ENOUGH

Medicare is a federal program to help people over sixty-five pay their health care bills, but it was never intended to pay all of those bills. This means you'll probably have to pay most of your medical bills some other way. This could result in large medical bills for you to pay if you require a long treatment program for a serious condition. A person age sixty-five or over and able to afford coverage to supplement Medicare should consider these options:

- You can pay out of your own personal savings. This is called paying out of pocket. But since you don't know in advance how large your medical bills will be, it's probably not a good idea to rely on your savings to pay for everything Medicare doesn't cover.
- You can arrange to carry over the health insurance you had before you turned sixty-five—either a group policy you got as a fringe benefit on the

job, or an individual policy. Some policies can be continued after age sixty-five; others can't. If yours can, this is often your best bet. Your coverage is likely to be more comprehensive than you could get on your own, and since you're continuing a policy rather than starting a new one, you don't have to worry about any waiting periods.

- You might be able to get a major medical policy, which gives you broad coverage of most medical expenses, including hospitalization, physicians' care, and prescription drugs. With major medical policies, you pay a certain amount of your medical bills every year yourself (such as the first $50 or $100); this is called the deductible. Many major medical policies will pay 80 percent of almost all your health care expenses after the deductible.

  Major medical policies can be good buys. Unfortunately, they can rarely be purchased once you've passed age sixty-five. But you may be able to continue a major medical policy you had before age sixty-five.

- You might be able to join a health maintenance organization, or HMO. This is a group health care plan in which you pay a fixed amount each month or so, and use whatever health services you need at the HMO facility. Most HMO plans also provide coverage for hospitalization. If there is one near you, HMOs can be an excellent choice.

  Since HMO members must get most of their treatment at the HMO facilities, be sure before you join that you can get there and are satisfied with the service the HMO provides.

- You can buy a hospital indemnity policy, which pays a certain amount such as $20 or $40 for each day you are in the hospital. These policies are advertised in newspapers and on subway and bus billboards. Sometimes they're endorsed by celebrities. Often, they're sold by direct mail.

  Hospital indemnity policies have two major problems for consumers. First, they pay off only if you're hospitalized. It's possible to run up sizable medical bills without ever being in the hospital. Second, since the policies pay a fixed dollar amount per day, they don't keep up with rising health care costs. The typical hospital indemnity policy pays only 10 to 30 percent of average daily hospital costs.

- You can buy a policy specifically designed to fill the gaps of Medicare. These are called Medicare supplement policies, or Medigap policies. Medigap benefits are generally stated in terms of percentages rather than fixed dollar amounts; this means they keep up better with rising health care costs. If you can't carry over your previous insurance or join an HMO, Medigap policies will often be your best buy.

- If your income is low, you might be eligible for Medicaid. Medicaid and Medicare together will pay almost all your medical bills, with a few exceptions such as foot care and private duty nursing. To find out if you are eligible for Medicaid, call your County Department of Social Services. If you are eligible, you don't need any other health insurance policy.

No matter which choice you make, don't be deceived into thinking that all your health care bills will be covered by insurance. They won't. Some will be covered by Medicare, some will be covered by any additional insurance you buy, and some will still be left for you to pay out of pocket.

In general, try to stick to one policy. Some people, knowing that there are gaps in their insurance policy and in Medicare, run around buying two, three,

or four policies. They hope that if they buy enough health insurance policies, somehow their medical bills will be covered and they won't be a burden on their children.

This isn't the best way to buy health insurance. Even if you buy duplicate coverage, you probably will not get duplicate payments. Instead, the overlapping policies will probably each pay part of your expenses.

The best way to buy health insurance is to take your time and select the best policy you can find. Once you've done that, there's usually no point in spending extra money paying premiums on more than one policy.

When looking for supplemental insurance always comparison shop. There are many policies on the market today. Compare the costs and benefits of more than one company. The same basic benefits can vary in cost by hundreds of dollars. Write down information about different policies as it is explained to you, then talk to a trusted advisor to make your decision. Generally speaking, you should be looking for insurance that will pay for the deductibles and co-payments required by Medicare, and that will pay for health services you need when Medicare coverage reaches its limits. There are two important points to keep in mind when buying supplemental health insurance. First, don't buy duplicate coverage; most insurance policies have a clause that states that the policy will not cover expenses covered under another policy. Second, make sure you buy a comprehensive policy.

Medicare/Private Insurance Checklist

When considering the purchase of private health insurance to supplement Medicare, you should compare different policies for what they cover and what they cost. Following are checklists for several different kinds of policies. By completing a checklist for each policy you are considering and comparing the results, you will be able to determine how well each kind of policy meets your health insurance needs.

I — Medicare Supplement Policies—Use this checklist for insurance policies that promise to pay "all the expenses that Medicare does not pay" or that promise to pay "all the gaps in Medicare." By checking the "yes" and "no" blocks for each of the listed items that Medicare does not cover and answering the other questions, you will be able to see at a glance just how well the proposed policy can help you meet the health care expenses Medicare does not pay.

NAME OF COMPANY_____ PREMIUM $_____

POLICY #_____

NOT COVERED BY MEDICARE (fill in current figures available from your local Social Security office)	COVERED BY PROPOSED POLICY		WHAT DOES PROPOSED POLICY PAY
	YES	NO	
Cost of inpatient hospitalization $_____Day 1 cost (the deductible) $_____Days 2–15 cost $_____Days 16–60 cost $_____Days 61–90 cost			
$_____a day for inpatient hospital services for each "reserve" day used (can be used up to a total of 60 days, whenever you need more than 90 days in a benefit period)			
Over 150 days of inpatient hospital services in a benefit period (over 90 days if you have used all your "reserve" days)			
$_____a day for the 21st through 100th day in a benefit period for inpatient services in a skilled nursing facility			
Over 100 days of inpatient skilled nursing facility care in a benefit period			
Nursing home care in other than a skilled nursing facility			
Private room in a hospital or skilled nursing facility (except when medically necessary)			
Private duty nurses in a hospital or skilled nursing facility			
The first 3 pints of blood under either Medicare hospital or medical insurance			

NOT COVERED BY MEDICARE	COVERED BY PROPOSED POLICY YES NO	WHAT DOES PROPOSED POLICY PAY
(fill in current figures available from your local Social Security office)		
The first $_____ of doctor bills and other medical services and supplies under Medicare medical insurance (the medical insurance annual deductible)		
After the first _____ percent of the amount approved by Medicare ("reasonable charge") for:		
Doctor's bills		
Outpatient hospital services		
Outpatient physical therapy and speech pathology services		
Other medical services and supplies		
Charges above the amount approved by Medicare in non-assignment cases		
Drugs and medicines you buy yourself		
Eyeglasses (except after cataract surgery)		
Hearing aids		
Dental care		
Medical care outside the United States (except under certain conditions in Canada and Mexico)		

Are there any additional benefits the proposed policy pays?   YES____ NO____
If yes, describe. _____
_____
_____
_____

II — Hospital Indemnity Policy—Use this checklist for insurance policies that promise to pay "cash" for each day you are a hospital inpatient. Remember that hospital indemnity policies always pay on a per-day basis. Do not be misled by policies that advertise, for example, "$1,500 per month." That is only about $50 a day and the policy will not pay for any days you are not in the hospital. In addition, be sure you know on what day of your stay the daily payments begin and whether there is a maximum number of days or total amount that can be paid.

NAME OF COMPANY_____ PREMIUM $_____

POLICY #_____

    a. What is the daily payment rate?　　$_____per day
    b. On what day of a hospital stay do payments begin? _____
    c. What is the maximum number of days the policy will pay?_____
    d. Is there a maximum payment provision?　　　　YES____ NO____
       If yes, what is the maximum amount? _____
    e. Are there any excluded illnesses? If yes, describe.　　YES____ NO____

    f. Are there any benefits in addition to the daily　　YES____ NO____
       payment rate? If yes, describe.

    III — Nursing Home Policies—Use this checklist for insurance policies that promise to pay for "nursing home" care. Nursing home policies are usually very limited and exclude care that most people associate with the phrase "nursing home." Be sure you know what kind of nursing home care is covered. Most nursing home policies cover only medically necessary care in a Medicare-certified skilled nursing facility, and do not cover custodial or long-term care in either a skilled nursing facility or other type of nursing home.

NAME OF COMPANY_____ PREMIUM $_____

POLICY #_____

    a. Does the policy cover care in facilities
       other than skilled nursing facilities?　　　　YES____ NO____
       If yes, what other kinds of nursing homes?

    b. Does the policy cover your stay in a skilled nursing facility or other nursing home when the care you need is primarily custodial care, that is, mainly personal care, such as help in feeding, dressing, getting in and out of bed, and taking medicine?　　　　YES____ NO____
       If yes, under what conditions and for how long will the policy pay for such care?

    c. Are there any excluded illnesses? If yes, describe.　YES____ NO____

NOTE: Don't buy specific disease policies (which are illegal in some states); they are rarely worth the cost, and sometimes the insurer reneges on payment.

THE HEALTH CARE SYSTEM

Our health care system is a complex and expensive one. If you plan to stay where you are now living, you may already know how and where you can receive health services in the community, including hospitals, doctors, clinics, dentists, nursing homes, and other health-related services. If your community has a local Area Agency on Aging you may obtain more information from them. Many areas publish information about the health care system that could prove of much value when the need arises.

If you plan to move to a new location when you retire, one of your prime concerns should be to learn what health services are available.

Choosing a Physician

There are a number of sources of information available to help you choose a physician. One of these is to ask friends for their recommendation. If you need the services of a specialist, your family physician may be able to recommend a competent colleague. Nurses also may be able to advise you. In addition, the local medical society usually maintains a list of physicians who are accepting new patients. Such a list will be maintained on a rotating basis, however. You are given the name of the physician at the top of the list, not information on competency, fees, or other factors that may be of concern to you. The yellow pages of the telephone directory may also list physicians both alphabetically and by specialty.

The following checklist may help you in finding a new doctor or dentist or in evaluating your present one.

1. Are you comfortable with your doctor? Do you feel you can openly discuss your problems, including very personal concerns?
2. Do you believe your doctor will stand by you, no matter how difficult your problems become?
3. Does your doctor listen to you and answer all your questions about the causes and treatment of your physical problems? Is he or she vague, impatient, or unwilling to discuss your situation?
4. Does your doctor take a thorough medical history and ask you about past physical and emotional problems, family medical history, drugs you are taking, and other matters affecting your health?
5. Does your doctor seem to prescribe drugs automatically rather than deal with the causes of your medical problems?
6. Does your doctor attribute your problems to "old age"?

Remember, a good doctor–patient relationship is based upon mutual respect and open communication. You owe your physician cooperation and honesty, and you owe yourself a continuing interest in seeking the best available medical care.

Purchasing Prescription Drugs

Many retired people find it necessary, because of a chronic condition, to purchase certain prescription drugs continually. If you are in this category you know how expensive this can be.

The price of a particular prescription drug often varies a good deal from pharmacy to pharmacy. It pays, therefore, to shop around for the best price. There are other factors to consider too when choosing a pharmacy, such as convenient location, the quality of service provided, availability of home delivery services, and whether or not a discount is offered to older adults. To protect yourself, it's always a good idea to count the number of tablets or capsules given to you by the pharmacist to make sure you get what you pay for.

Some states have what are known as generic drug laws. The purpose of such laws is to enable consumers to purchase certain drugs under their less expensive generic name, rather than by the more expensive brand name. The generic name of a drug is its chemical name, while the brand name is the trade name under which it is often advertised and sold. There are usually significant, and sometimes vast, differences in price between generic and brand name drugs even though they may be equivalent chemically and in the way they affect your body. To learn more about these laws, ask your physician or pharmacist.

COMMUNITY HEALTH SERVICES

If you are a long-time resident of your community, you are probably aware of area hospital services. But you may want to investigate other services, such as walk-in clinics and outpatient hospital services.

HOME HEALTH CARE

"When can I go home?" is probably the question most often asked by patients recovering from a serious illness or injury. They eagerly anticipate returning to comforting surroundings and relaxing back into the familiar routines of daily life.

Staying home is the wish of many people with an injury, a long-term, progressive illness, a terminal disease, or a disabling condition. Many people who are ill still wish to live as independently as possible. Everyone deserves the choice to live their lives as they wish.

Home care is not a new form of care; in fact, it is the oldest. Although 80 percent of all home care is provided by families, there is often a need for

THE WIZARD OF ID   **by Brant parker and Johnny hart**

in-home health care services from community organizations to provide the necessary help, support, guidance, or relief to the family to allow the patient to remain at home.

Organizations offering assistance in home health care build on the resources of the individual and family. Home care can be provided to people who are ill, at risk, frail, disabled, or incapacitated. Many kinds of illnesses and injuries, both short- and long-term, can be successfully cared for in the home. Home care can include short-term assistance (such as help after a stroke or back injury) or long-term assistance (such as care for a blind diabetic).

The familiar home setting often speeds recovery from an illness or injury or delays deterioration of a chronic condition. Some persons prefer to spend their last days in the privacy and comfort of their own home. Home health care professionals will help the family members improve the quality of life for the dying person when the length of life cannot be extended.

There are four levels of health care in the home: *maintenance care* to support one's present level of health and independence; *preventive care* to reduce future episodes of illness; *treatment* to care for specific problems; and *rehabilitation* to regain a previous level of health. The home care plan for each person is different, depending on need.

Maintenance care offers a wide variety of home services that enable a handicapped or frail person to remain in their own home. It may be homemaker service several hours a week or volunteers who do household chores for those people who cannot do them themselves. Shopper/escort services may be available to assist with grocery shopping, banking, and running errands. Home-delivered meals provide two meals daily for those unable to cook for themselves. Specialized transportation provides bus service to handicapped and older persons in the city or in outlying areas.

Preventive care includes various forms of health education, teaching, and guidance by skilled professionals. Families can be guided in the care of the patient, from bathing techniques to the proper administration of medications. Patient and family education on special diets is also provided.

Home health aides provide routine personal care. The needs of the patient dictate the level of skilled nursing care that is provided.

Many treatments prescribed by a physician can be effectively performed in the home. Registered nurses perform ongoing assessments of the patient's status and communicate with a physician regularly. Medical home care equipment is also available through loan closets and/or retail suppliers. Laboratory work may be necessary and these services can also be provided in the home.

In addition to physical care, family support and guidance helps patients and families cope with difficult adjustments. Rehabilitation care includes the services of physical, occupational, speech, and respiratory therapists. They work closely with the patient and family to restore health to its optimum level.

Information on obtaining home health care may be obtained from a variety of sources. Hospital discharge planners work closely with families to obtain this form of care. Home care services work hand in hand with inpatient services, enabling earlier discharges and aiding in a smooth transition to the home.

A physician's referral may be required for some forms of home care. However, support services may also be initiated by the family simply contacting a home care organization.

Payment for home care services can be handled through Medicaid, Medicare, and some forms of private insurance. Coverage is complex and may be limited. Everyone should check their current insurance policies for home health care coverage. Home health care may be less costly than hospital fees or the cost of a long stay in a nursing home or other institution; it is viewed by many as one way to cut the skyrocketing cost of health care in the United States.

Sometimes, home health care is impossible, due to the severity of the illness, safety issues, limited funding, or family support. Home health care is not for everyone. But it can be a health incentive and a positive experience for all involved. Health care provided among family and friends and in an encouraging, familiar, and comfortable environment can create a feeling of independence for a person undergoing a difficult experience.

Health is one of the primary areas of concern to almost everyone. This is especially true for those approaching retirement because middle-aged people and older adults experience chronic health problems more often than those who are younger.

The best way to take care of your health is to take steps that help keep a health problem from starting. These include maintaining a proper balance of exercise and rest, good nutrition, a healthy mental attitude, avoiding or minimizing use of tobacco and alcohol, and using medicines wisely.

Prevention also means early detection, the willingness to admit that a health problem may be present, and taking positive steps to see that an existing health problem does not ruin the other aspects of a healthy life.

SITUATIONS TO CONSIDER

Following are a number of situations that pose problems related to the subject of this chapter. There are no right or wrong "answers" to these situations. They are presented simply to stimulate your thinking about retirement and to emphasize certain aspects of retirement planning. It is not necessary to arrive at any particular conclusion about each case.

It's a good idea for couples to review the situations separately and then share their thoughts. If you are single, perhaps you have a friend, relative, or clergyman with whom you can exchange ideas. Discussing situations like these can help to clarify key aspects of retirement planning and will enable you to become more in tune with your feelings and those of others.

Situation 1: On Again, Off Again

Nora estimates that throughout her life she has "lost" about three hundred pounds. Every time she goes on a diet she loses weight, then gains it right back when she goes off the diet. She has tried the egg diet, the grapefruit diet, the water diet, and about a half dozen other "latest" diets. None of them seem to work permanently for her. She very much wants to lose the thirty-five pounds of excess baggage. What should she do?

Thoughts to Consider

1. Is there anything wrong with "fad" diets as long as you lose the weight? If so, what?

A DAILY FOOD GUIDE

You can get the kinds of food that make up nutritious meals by using this simple food guide.

MILK GROUP

Milk is our leading source of calcium, which is needed for bones and teeth. Milk also provides protein, riboflavin, vitamin A, and many other nutrients.

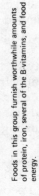

FOODS INCLUDED

Milk: fluid whole, skim, lowfat, evaporated, dry, and buttermilk.

Milk alternatives on the basis of calcium content are:

Cheddar-type cheese, 1-inch cube = 1/2 cup milk
Cream cheese, 2 tablespoons = 1 tablespoon milk
Cottage cheese, 1/2 cup = 1/3 cup milk
Ice cream, 1/2 cup = 1/4 cup milk
Ice milk, 1/2 cup = 2/5 cup milk

AMOUNTS RECOMMENDED

Use 2 or more cups of milk or the equivalent in a milk alternate, every day.

VEGETABLE-FRUIT GROUP

Vegetables and fruits are valuable chiefly because of the vitamins and minerals they contain. The guide emphasizes those that are valuable as sources of vitamin C and vitamin A.

Vitamin C is needed for healthy gums and body tissues. Vitamin A is needed for growth, normal vision, and healthy condition of the skin.

FOODS INCLUDED

All vegetables and fruits.

Sources of vitamin C

cantaloupe	collards
grapefruit	green pepper
honeydew melon	kale
lemon	potato
orange	sweet potato
raw strawberries	raw cabbage
tangerine	spinach
watermelon	sweet red pepper
asparagus tips	tomato
broccoli	turnip greens
brussels sprouts	

Sources of vitamin A

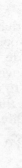

apricots	chard
broccoli	pumpkin
cantaloup	spinach
carrots	sweet potato
	turnip greens
	winter squash
	other dark green leaves

AMOUNTS RECOMMENDED

Choose 4 or more servings daily including:
1 serving of a source of vitamin C.
1 serving, at least every other day, of a source of vitamin A. If the food chosen for vitamin C is also a source of vitamin A, the additional serving of a vitamin A food may be omitted.
2 or more servings of any vegetable or fruit, including those that are valuable for vitamin C and vitamin A.

Count as a serving: 1/2 cup of vegetables or fruit; or a portion as ordinarily served, such as one medium apple, banana, orange, or potato, half a medium grapefruit or cantaloup, or the juice of one lemon.

MEAT GROUP

Foods in this group are valued for their protein, which is needed for growth and repair of muscle, organs, blood, skin, and hair. These foods also provide iron, thiamin, riboflavin, niacin, and several other nutrients.

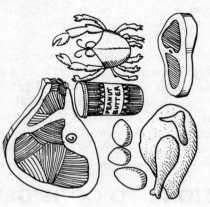

FOODS INCLUDED

Beef, veal, lamb, pork, organ meats such as liver, heart, and kidney; poultry and eggs; fish and shellfish; meat alternates — dry beans, dry peas, lentils, and peanut butter.

AMOUNTS RECOMMENDED

Choose 2 or more servings every day.

Count as a serving: 2 to 3 ounces (without bone) of lean cooked meat, poultry, or fish. Equivalent in protein to 2 ounces meat are 2 eggs; 1 cup cooked beans, dry peas, or lentils; 4 tablespoons peanut butter.

BREAD-CEREAL GROUP

Foods in this group furnish worthwhile amounts of protein, iron, several of the B-vitamins, and food energy.

FOODS INCLUDED

All breads and cereals that are whole grain, enriched, or restored. Check labels to be sure.

This group includes:

breads	macaroni
cooked cereals	spaghetti
ready-to-eat cereals	noodles
cornmeal	rice
crackers	rolled oats
flour	parboiled rice and wheat
grits	

and quick breads and other baked goods if made with whole grain or enriched flour.

Check labels to be sure products are whole grain, enriched, or restored.

AMOUNTS RECOMMENDED

Choose 4 or more servings daily. If no cereals are chosen, have an extra serving of breads or baked goods.

Count as a serving: 1 slice of bread; 1 ounce ready-to-eat cereal; 1/2 to 3/4 cup cooked cereal, cornmeal, grits, macaroni, noodles, rice, or spaghetti.

THE WIZARD OF ID   by Brant parker and Johnny hart

2. Other than better looks, list some of the chief benefits of obtaining your optimum weight.
   (1)
   (2)
   (3)
3. Why are so many people overweight?
4. Is being overweight dangerous? Why?
5. Are there some good weight-reducing programs in your community? How do they work?

Situation 2: How Much Smoking Is Too Much?

For most of his adult life, Ron has smoked one to two packs of cigarettes a day. After a recent chest cold, he is beginning to become more concerned about the cumulative effects of his smoking. Other than shortness of breath during physical activity and a cough when he arises in the morning, he feels fine. He knows that he should cut down, but doesn't feel he can quit. How can Ron save his health, or is it too late?

Thoughts to Consider

1. What are some of the health dangers Ron might face?
2. If Ron were a good friend of yours, how might you help him quit smoking?
3. What resources are available to Ron in your community if he decides to quit?

Situation 3: Heart Attack?

After a tense day at the office and a big dinner, Harry was up almost all night with what felt like indigestion and heartburn. He also felt a slight tingling in his left arm and is worried that it might be something serious. How should Harry handle this experience?

Thoughts to Consider

1. Has anyone you know ever had symptoms like Harry? How did they handle that experience?
2. What symptoms would you look for as signs of a heart attack?

3. Can a person who has a heart condition lead a normal life? What are some of the activities a person with a heart condition can engage in?
4. What kinds of activities should be avoided by people with a heart condition?
5. If a person has a heart attack in your presence, what should you do?
6. What are the "risk factors" associated with heart disease? What steps can you take to find out more about heart attacks and heart disease?

Situation 4: The Doctor Won't Talk

For some time Martin has not been feeling up to par. He has visited his physician twice recently but each time she has been vague as to what his problem might actually be. At the last visit she suggested that he undergo some tests, then consider the possibility of surgery. Martin is uncomfortable with the whole situation. Every time he asks questions his physician either becomes impatient or answers in medical terms he doesn't understand. What would you do if you were Martin?

Thoughts to Consider

1. Why do you think some physicians fail to talk openly with their patients?
2. Would you advise Martin to get a second opinion?
3. What are some things you might suggest to Martin to develop better patient-physician communication?
4. What are some things you might do to strengthen your relationship with your physician?

Situation 5: The Exercise Routine

John is five years from retirement and wants to be healthy and active after retirement. He recently had an A-OK physical and just watched a TV program on physical fitness. He has decided that, starting tomorrow morning, he is going to jog before breakfast, play handball at the "Y" during lunch hour, and do some calisthenics before going to bed. What do you think?

Thoughts to Consider

1. Do you think it's wise for John to take on such a vigorous exercise routine without first completing a warm-up exercise routine suggested by his physician?
2. Do you exercise regularly? How often? Doing what?
3. Why don't more people exercise?
4. If you don't exercise, what are some ways you might start?
5. What are some things that might prevent you from exercising?

REFERENCES AND RESOURCES

The Alcoholic American. National Association of Blue Shield Plans, 1973.

Cooking for Two (Revised 1974). U.S. Department of Agriculture. Available from the Superintendent of Documents, U.S. Government Printing Office, Washington, DC 20402.

Costales, Claire, and Jo Berry. *Alcoholism: The Way Back to Reality*. Ventura, Calif.: Regal Books, 1980.

Coudert, Jo. *Alcoholic in Your Life*. Briarcliff Manor, N.Y.: Stein & Day, 1981.

Cramer, Quenton. *Medical Tips for the Pre-Retiree and Retiree*. New York: Vantage Press, 1982.

Food and Fitness: Blue Print for Health. Vol. XXIV, No. 1. Chicago: Blue Cross Assoc., 1973.

Garnet, Eva D. *Movement Is Life: A Holistic Approach to Exercise for Older Adults*. Princeton: Princeton Book Co., 1982.

Gordon, Michael. *Old Enough to Feel Better: A Medical Guide for Seniors*. Radnor, Pa.: Chilton Book Co., 1981.

A Guide for Food and Nutrition in the Later Years. Oakland, Calif.: Society for Nutrition Education (1736 Franklin St., 9th Floor, 94612), 1980.

Guide to Home and Personal Security and *Guide for Dynamic Fitness*. Washington, D.C.: Action for Independent Maturity (1909 K St., N.W., 20006).

Kayne, Ronald C., ed. *Drugs and the Elderly*. University Park, Calif.: U.S.C. Gerontology Center, 1978.

Nutrition Labeling. Information Bulletin No. 382, U.S. Department of Agriculture, 1975. Available from the Superintendent of Documents, U.S. Government Printing Office, Washington, DC 20402.

Warner-Reitz, Anne, and Carolyn Grothe. *Healthy Life Style for Seniors: An Inter-Disciplinary Approach to Healthy Aging*. New York: Meals For Millions, Freedom From Hunger (815 2nd Ave., Suite 1001, 10017), 1981.

Your Retirement Food Guide, Your Retirement Health Guide, and *Your Retirement Safety Guide*. Washington, D.C.: American Association of Retired Persons (1909 K St., N.W., 20006).

The local office of the Social Security Administration provides free booklets on Medicare and Medicaid.

Literature is also available from local chapters of those organizations concerned with specific health problems, such as the American Cancer Society and the American Lung Association.

Chapter 3
Legal Affairs

CHAPTER 3 WARM-UP

Before reading "Legal Affairs," test your general knowledge of the subject by placing a check mark next to the answer you prefer. Check the key at the end to find the right answer.

1. All lawyers charge the same fees for certain standard services.   True_____ False_____
2. Co-signing a note can obligate you to pay.   True_____ False_____
3. Most "standard legal documents" are safe to sign without a lawyer's advice.   True_____ False_____
4. Everyone needs a will.   True_____ False_____
5. Probate applies only to larger estates.   True_____ False_____
6. You don't have to have a large estate to have a trust.   True_____ False_____
7. Community property laws give each spouse one-half ownership of combined property.   True_____ False_____
8. Older adults are federally protected from age discrimination in the fields of employment and credit.   True_____ False_____
9. Tenancy by the entirety is limited to husband/wife ownership.   True_____ False_____
10. Once a will is made it usually isn't revised.   True_____ False_____

Key: 1. (F), 2. (T), 3. (F), 4. (T), 5. (F), 6. (T), 7. (T), 8. (T), 9. (T), 10. (F).

WHO NEEDS A LAWYER?

Who needs a lawyer? Almost everyone! Here are two illustrations out of many that show how getting early legal advice could have saved time, money, and anguish.

Joe had been a good, kind neighbor, a model husband and father who worked hard to provide for his family until he died. His death aroused deep sorrow and regret. Joe was dearly missed. There was also regret of another sort that lingered on and on—and on. Because Joe never made a will. No one knew where his important papers were, nor was anyone quite sure what Joe's assets were. Despite his many fine qualities, Joe had avoided what he had not understood—the law, and the importance of seeing a lawyer. Only when he had bought a house many years ago did Joe have anything to do with a lawyer. So it was that when he died, it took two years to settle his estate, which delayed transfer of his assets to his family and reduced the value of the final amount substantially because of the added administrative cost.

John went into business with a friend. They were excited about the new venture and its opportunities, but talked little about the details of their relationship. The business prospered for a time, but eventually ran into management difficulties, with each partner blaming the other. They finally sought the help of a lawyer and drew up a belated, but sorely needed, partnership agreement.

The purpose of this chapter is to show you how to avoid these kinds of troubles by knowing when to consult a lawyer. We'll review the basic legal planning you should be doing, such as the preparation of a will, and we'll review trusts, contracts, buying and selling a home, and several other legal transactions for which a lawyer may be needed.

Legal "mistakes" can cost us dearly. It's important to know enough about the law to protect our rights, and it's equally important to know that in some areas, our own knowledge is not enough.

Unfortunately, many people don't realize how important having a lawyer is. They often feel their dealings are too small and insignificant to bother with consulting an attorney. Some want to avoid paying the high fees they think a lawyer will charge. Others feel awkward about sharing personal (and, often, emotional) concerns with a "stranger." Still others, like Joe in the introduction, will ignore anything they don't understand.

Take the time to select a competent lawyer carefully. You probably won't need the lawyer on a day-to-day basis, but when you do need one, he or she will be there.

CHOOSING A LAWYER

Finding a lawyer who is right for you usually takes some time. Fortunately, most people can afford to take the time since they are looking for a lawyer to advise them *before* things happen that require an attorney's attention. This is obviously preferred to a last-minute rush job when you are suddenly in a jam.

How do you go about finding a good lawyer: one who meets your particular needs, is sympathetic to your situation, and doesn't charge more than you can afford?

One good way to start is by talking to people and finding satisfied customers. Start your investigation by asking people you know for recommendations. Friends and relatives may have suggestions or experiences with lawyers to share. A banker, union representative, employer, or company lawyer might also have suggestions.

A "good" lawyer is one who meets your needs. When you speak to people about attorneys, ask some of these questions:

1. What kind of work did the lawyer perform?
2. What field (if any) does the lawyer specialize in?
3. Was the work done well and on time?
4. How expensive was it?
5. Did the lawyer work on a fixed fee basis, or charge by time and material?

There are several other sources that are also available to you. In many communities, the local Bar Association sponsors a lawyer reference service. It will provide a list of local lawyers for you to choose from. You can arrange for an initial conference at a small fee with one or several of these lawyers, and make your decision from there.

If you think you are unable to afford a lawyer, you may want to look into nonprofit legal assistance programs. Although these are not available in all communities, they are in many. These clinics offer flat rates for designated services. In addition, law schools often sponsor clinics where students, under proper supervision, give legal advice. And for those in serious financial difficulty, Legal Aid societies or Legal Assistance Corporations offer free legal help, in cooperation with local Bar Associations.

The Martindale-Hubbell Law Directory rates certain credentials of all practicing lawyers. Although the publication is generally sold only to lawyers, it is available at many public libraries and law libraries. The directory is updated yearly.

Lawyers may now advertise their services. In states that recognize fields of specialization, a lawyer may include that information in his or her advertising. In states that do not recognize specializations, a lawyer may state that he or she restricts practice to certain fields.

Many people do not know what to expect when they visit a law office. What will it be like? What am I expected to do? A law office is just like any other business office. You should first make an appointment. Lawyers have demands on their time and usually keep tight schedules. During your first visit a lawyer should do a preliminary evaluation of your problem and discuss with you what needs to be done.

Don't hesitate to talk frankly about charges. If you think the proposed charges are too high, say so, or ask for an itemization of charges and negotiate. Many lawyers will negotiate their fees, which may put legal services within your budget.

Lawyers usually charge on the basis of how much time your particular situation may need. This includes not only the time spent with you, but also time spent by the office staff working on your case. Sometimes, lawyers will charge a flat fee for certain kinds of services, such as the handling of a real estate transaction, the drawing up of a will, or probating an estate. In certain cases lawyers receive a percentage of the amount their client collects through awards of the court. There are even times where they may not receive any fee if the case is lost. While everyone hears about great sums of money lawyers receive for handling unusual or difficult cases, lawyers' fees are generally very reasonable for the work they perform.

There are certain kinds of work lawyers do for which their fee is subject to approval by the courts or a governmental agency. In general, lawyers' fees are controlled in cases involving guardianships and estates of deceased persons and in proceedings concerning certain kinds of retirement benefits, such as Social Security.

Sometimes you may pay just for receiving advice from a lawyer. But giving advice before something happens may be the most valuable service a lawyer can perform. Getting things straightened out before problems arise can save you money later on.

It also pays to be a good client. Understanding what lawyers have to offer and the limits they cannot go beyond will help maintain the best relationship possible. A lawyer wants you to be satisfied with his or her services. Give him or her the chance to explain, and don't hesitate to ask questions. If you do have a problem with an attorney or the service you received, contact your local Bar Association. It will investigate the matter and respond to your complaint.

WHEN TO SEE A LAWYER

A lawyer is there to give you advice concerning legal matters that affect you and, if necessary, to use legal procedures to handle these matters. There are a number of decisions you'll be making both before and during retirement. Making a decision that's right for you is sometimes not an easy thing to do. You may want to talk to family members, friends, and professionals in the community about these decisions. Make sure you don't forget to include your lawyer, especially if a course of action has legal implications that must be considered.

In fact, it's a good idea to have a periodic legal "checkup." Just as you should go to a doctor periodically for a physical examination, so should you make it a point to visit your lawyer. In this way your lawyer will become familiar with your situation and be alerted to any problems that may come up.

Periodic consultations are also a good idea because laws and circumstances change almost yearly. Definitely consult your lawyer when a major change is occurring in your life. This could be a death, marriage, divorce, birth, or a change in your financial situation. If you move to a new state it's also a good

idea to consult a lawyer. The laws of each state vary and what may be a valid last will and testament in one state may not be in another. There are also other important legal matters that may need to be considered when you move across state lines.

The law is there to help you. So use it when you need to and let it serve you.

THE IMPORTANCE OF A WILL

"Why do I need a will? I don't have a big estate."

"Doesn't it cost a lot to make a will? I'm not sure I would know what I want anyway."

Perhaps such thoughts crossed the mind of Joe, the man described in the introduction who left his family with a complicated mess. A will would have eliminated much of the frustration Joe's family had to endure in straightening out his estate.

Three out of four people die without having made up a will. Most of these people probably assumed the courts would distribute their property as they would have, with most of the estate going to their spouse and the rest to their children. This is not always the case.

If you die intestate (without a will) many different things can happen. Property is not always automatically passed along to the most logical or appropriate person. The assumption that the court will do what is best for your family does not guarantee that the state will distribute your estate as you would have liked. Your daughter's need for college tuition, for example, may not even be considered by the court. When you die without a will, your estate is disposed of according to strict state laws. Though a husband who died without a will might have thought that all his possessions would automatically go to his wife, in the majority of states, the wife will get one half to one third of the estate, the remainder being divided among the deceased's children, parents, brothers, and sisters.

There is also additional time, expense, and paperwork involved in the distribution of unwilled assets. This delay and loss could be financially crippling to a family.

WHO NEEDS A WILL?

Everyone needs a will. Many people don't make out wills because they think they don't own enough; others refuse to acknowledge the inevitability of their own death.

Both a husband and wife should have a will. Take the example of Jack and Laura, married for twenty-five years. He had a will and she didn't. They assumed that since the majority of the assets were in Jack's name, Laura didn't need a will. He died and left everything to her. Laura died unexpectedly shortly after. All of their property was then distributed according to state laws, with heavy taxes paid. This situation created a lot of unnecessary family anguish and tension among the surviving family.

Married couples should also make sure their wills agree. Remember, wills are relatively inexpensive and can be redrawn from time to time. If, in that rare instance, a couple is killed in a common disaster, conflicting wills can complicate the settling of the estate.

Whether you have accumulated much over your lifetime or just have a few things you'd like certain people to have, you ought to put your wishes down in writing. Here are some reasons for making your will *now:*

1. It allows you to decide on the distribution of your belongings to meet your family's needs.
2. It can reduce taxes considerably.
3. It reduces probate time and costs—important to your family's financial well-being.
4. It gives you the opportunity to arrange a trust, if needed, under experienced financial management.
5. It enables you to decide who the executor will be.
6. It prevents distribution of your estate to persons you would not wish to include.

Making a Will

1. Choose a lawyer, if you don't already have one. Although it can be done, you are advised not to try to write your will without a lawyer's assistance. Books and sample wills provide some guidance for those who choose to make their own wills. However, the subtleties of language and fine points of the law are not likely to be within your knowledge. The will you prepare on your own may not stand up in court. For a relatively small cost, the lawyer's services are a bargain.
2. Determine your assets and who your beneficiaries should be. If you want certain people to have certain things, make a note of it. But do remember that the more complex the will, the higher the cost. At this point, you may want to consider getting additional professional planning help, especially if you have a large estate. An investment officer, estate planner, or accountant could help you save a great deal in taxes with a properly planned estate.
3. Choose an executor. The executor is responsible for administering the will and performing all related duties. He or she must:
   - compile an inventory of the estate (if it hasn't been done)
   - assume control over all of the deceased's personal property
   - identify and collect monies due the estate
   - pay estate taxes and expenses
   - have all properties appraised for tax purposes
   - pay all legacies named in the will
   - continuously report all developments to heirs and the courts.
   For his or her services, the executor gets a commission—a certain percentage of the estate. This commission may vary from state to state. Legal fees for assisting the executor vary and may either be based upon a percentage of the estate or a time and material charge.

   The executor should be a responsible, well-organized person. If you want to name your spouse, relative, or close friend as executor, be sure that person is capable of handling these responsibilities. You may want to name co-executors, with your lawyer or banker as one and your spouse or friend the other. You may also want to choose a substitute executor, should your executor die before you.

When no executor is named in the will, or when there is no will, the executor is chosen by the courts. Usually the surviving spouse is chosen. He or she gets administrative assistance from the lawyer working on the estate, or the lawyer who drew up the will.

4. Finalize the will. This is the area where your attorney's knowledge of the fine points of the law can make the difference between a valid will and one that doesn't stand up in court. As mentioned before, a lawyer is aware of the legal technicalities that must be adhered to. He or she will advise you on witnesses for your will and other matters necessary to make your will a legal document.

Revising the Will

Your will should be looked at every few years and revised according to changes in such circumstances as the following:

- Major changes in your estate's size or composition.
- Changes in tax laws or other regulations.
- Changes in your family and their needs.
- A move to another state.

If, after some time, the original will needs substantial revision (and many do) an entirely new will may have to be drawn up.

Probate

Probate laws direct the process of "proving" the will and distributing the estate to heirs. These laws also enable the state to collect its share through estate taxes. All of the deceased's assets are subject to probate, with the exception of certain properties in trusts, jointly owned property that goes directly to a survivor, life insurance that goes to a named beneficiary, and U.S. Savings Bonds with designated beneficiaries.

After someone dies, the will is brought to probate court for validation. The executor is then charged with paying off the debts, collecting what is owed to the estate, and distributing the remainder of the assets to the heirs.

Before the will is probated, funds in joint accounts may not be totally available to the surviving spouse. Therefore, it is often advisable for married people to establish accounts that will be available during the probate process.

PLANNING TOOLS

Checklist for Making a Will

Using this checklist, legal counsel can help you plan your will.

	Yes	No	Action to Be Taken	When?
1. Is your property in joint owner-ship?				
2. Should changes be made in the ownership of any of your assets for tax advantages?				

Checklist for Making a Will (*Continued*)

	Yes	No	Action to Be Taken	When?
3. Do you plan to sell your house?				
4. Can you identify (and appoint) an executor for your estate?				
5. Have you determined how your estate would be distributed in case of death of both in a common accident?				
6. Do you plan to have separate wills?				
7. Do you plan to establish a trust fund?				
8. Have you discussed and planned the distribution of assets in case a surviving spouse remarries?				
9. Do you plan to live in another state and, if so, have you been advised regarding its legal implications on your estate?				
10. Are there any special instructions or desires regarding your estate and your heirs that you wish to make known?				

Inventory and Location of Valuable Papers

The ability to locate your valuable papers quickly is vitally important to your survivors. Under location, clearly identify the specific desk and drawer, closet, box, etc. A careful annual scrutiny of this list is advisable.

Valuable Papers	Location	Last Review Date
1. Wills and Instructions (and copies)		
2. Funeral Directions		
3. Power of Attorney		
4. Insurance Policies (Life, Accident, etc.)		
5. Certificates (Marriage, Divorce, Birth, Death, etc.)		
6. Special Papers (Adoption, Naturalization, Passports)		
7. Diplomas and Educational Records		
8. Family Health Records (including insurance information)		
9. Resumes and Employment Records		

Valuable Papers	Location	Last Review Date
10. Stock Certificates & Bonds 11. Bank and Check Books 12. Income Tax Records 13. Canceled Checks and Stubs 14. Auto Records (Title, Repairs, Insurance) 15. Appliance Records (Guarantees, Instruction Books) 16. Real Estate Records (Deed, Mortgage, etc.) 17. Safe Deposit Box and Key 18. Social Security Information		

The Family Homestead

Your home is probably the largest single investment you make in your entire life. It is important, therefore, that adequate maintenance and repairs be carried out on the home not only to protect the investment but to assure the safety and convenience of the dwelling. If you should die, could your spouse perform routine maintenance and repairs? Would he or she know whom to contact if professional help is needed? Use the list below to provide the necessary information for your spouse if you should pass away or for yourself to protect against the loss of your spouse.

Original Purchase Price _____

Original Amount of Mortgage Loan _____

Name of Bank Holding Mortgage _____

Attorney for Closing _____

Mortgage Payment(s) Due _____

Mortgage Termination Date _____

Location of Important Papers:
  Mortgage _____
  Bond _____
  Deed _____
  Mortgage Insurance Certificate _____

When Property Taxes Are Due _____

Homeowners Insurance:
  Company _____
  Amount _____
  When Due _____
  Separate Contents Policy? _____

Utility Companies:
  Gas _____
  Electric _____
  Oil _____

Whom to Call If a Problem Arises:
  Electrician _____
  Plumber _____
  Roofing, siding, gutters _____
  Furnace repair and maintenance _____
  Carpenter _____
  Major appliances _____

For Renters:
  Landlord's Name _____
  When Rent Is Due _____
  When Lease Expires _____
  Location of Copy of Lease _____

The Family Car

In most families the husband assumes primary responsibility for the various tasks involved with the family car, such as registration, insurance, maintenance, and repairs. Problems can arise for a widow if she is unprepared to assume this responsibility. Below is a form that provides a convenient place to record necessary facts about the car and insurance and documents connected with it. It may be wise to complete the form now and update it periodically as changes occur.

	Car 1	Car 2
Make	_____	_____
Model	_____	_____
Year	_____	_____
Vehicle Identification Number	_____	_____
Registration Expires	_____	_____
Inspection Date	_____	_____
Original Purchase:		
Date	_____	_____
Dealer	_____	_____
Purchase Price	_____	_____
Insurance:		
Company	_____	_____
Agent	_____	_____
Amount of Personal Liability Coverage	_____	_____

	Car 1	Car 2
Amount of Property Damage Coverage	_____	_____
Collision Deductible Amount	_____	_____
Annual Premium	_____	_____

Location of Documents:

	Car 1	Car 2
Bill of Sale	_____	_____
Registration	_____	_____
Insurance Identification Card	_____	_____
Insurance Policy	_____	_____
Guarantees/Warranties/Receipts	_____	_____

Necessary Maintenance (How Often):

	Car 1	Car 2
Oil Change	_____	_____
Lubrication	_____	_____
Tune-Up	_____	_____
Brake Check	_____	_____
Tire Check	_____	_____
Wheel Alignment	_____	_____
Transmission Check	_____	_____

Service and Repairs (Whom to Call):

	Car 1	Car 2
Advice	_____	_____
Maintenance	_____	_____
Repairs	_____	_____
Body Work	_____	_____
Towing Service	_____	_____
Key Number (If Replacement Is Needed)	_____	_____
Location of Spare Ignition Key	_____	_____
Name of Auto Loan Company	_____	_____
Monthly Payment Due	_____	_____
Final Payment Date	_____	_____
Life Insurance on Auto Loan	_____	_____

ESTATE PLANNING

Your estate is your net worth, the sum total of your assets minus your debts. Careful planning in this area can do much to reduce taxes on your estate. And, like the will, estate planning is a tool that will let you control who your money goes to and what purpose it serves after your death.

Your estate planning options will depend on the size of your estate and how you would like to see your assets distributed. Your lawyer (and financial advisor) will explain the following information.

Estate Taxes

Estate taxation is a highly complex subject. What we present here are just the basics of what you should know about estate taxation. Your lawyer will be able to give you more specific information that applies to your own situation. Also be aware that these laws change frequently, so be sure the information you are receiving (whether it be here or elsewhere) is up-to-date.

Prior to 1982, the estate tax marital deduction was limited to $250,000 or 50 percent of the adjusted gross estate, whichever was larger. Now there is no limit on the amount that can be transferred to a spouse free of tax.

Current law exempts gifts of $10,000 per year to each donee ($20,000 for a married couple) from the unified gift and estate tax. So your ability to transfer property or cash to members of your family, undiminished by taxes, is greater than ever before.

Also, the total value of estates escaping federal gift or estate taxes has increased dramatically:

Year	Unified Credit Estate Exemption
1984	$325,000
1985	$400,000
1986	$500,000
1987 and beyond	$600,000

Estates not taxable by reason of this federal exemption will not be required, in general, to file a federal tax return.

The annual federal tax exclusion for gifts is $10,000 ($20,000 for gifts by both husband and wife). Gift tax exclusion for amounts paid for school tuition and medical care are unlimited and are in addition to the $10,000/$20,000 gift exclusion.

Since laws and interpretation of laws often change, an attorney should be consulted in each individual case. State law also may not precisely match federal law.

Trusts

Contrary to what you might think, you do not have to have a very large estate to have a trust. However, if your estate is very small you probably won't want to deal with the legal and managerial expenses that a trust involves.

A trust is an arrangement in which your assets are controlled by a trustee (usually, the trust department of a bank), in a manner you can dictate. Different types of trusts serve different purposes. Your attorney will help you determine which one best fits your needs.

The Living Trust

A living trust is just what it says. While you are alive, you arrange your assets to be managed and controlled (as you describe). The trustee has the responsibility to increase the assets through good investments and to meet the financial obligations of the estate. The trustee receives a fee for this service.

THE WIZARD OF ID   by Brant parker and Johnny hart

If you create a revocable living trust you have the opportunity to observe it in operation and make changes or cancel it. However, because you reserve the right to cancel it, it is considered part of your estate when you die (and is therefore subject to taxes) unless you change it to another kind of trust. The irrevocable living trust cannot be changed or canceled, and it is not considered part of your estate when you die. Either of these kinds of trusts can be terminated upon death or continue as testamentary trusts.

Living trusts are free from probate court account and so are not publicly exposed. You can also set up a living trust for yourself as a means of accumulating additional retirement income.

The Testamentary Trust

This kind of trust is established by the will and becomes effective on your death. It is usually best suited for people with larger estates. Since your property doesn't pass immediately to your heirs, it is not subject to inheritance taxes. If your beneficiaries are inexperienced in financial affairs, or if your estate tax is expected to be sizable, this kind of trust is something you should consider. Those with larger estates might want to set up two kinds of trusts: a marital trust and a nonmarital trust. The surviving spouse can receive income from both trusts and have full control over the marital trust. Upon the death of the surviving spouse, the nonmarital trust passes directly to the heirs and the marital trust portion passes on as directed by the surviving spouse (through a will or the terms of a trust).

The Insurance Trust

Often, the largest potential asset a person has is an insurance policy. This policy is normally considered part of the taxable estate. A life insurance trust, which is set up while you are still living, is designed to control the way in which the insurance money is to be preserved for the beneficiaries and to reduce estate taxes. Other assets of the estate may be included as part of the insurance trust. One of the prime benefits of a trust is the flexibility it can have. You can arrange a trust that can be "invaded" by its benefactor for financial emergencies or for any other reason you designate. The proceeds of the trust can also be designated for a specific purpose, such as a grandchild's college education.

THE WIZARD OF ID   **by Brant parker and Johnny hart**

PROPERTY OWNERSHIP

How your ownership is stated may affect your taxes, the probation of your will, or both. The "best" type of ownership will vary with individual circumstances. Check your deed and see how it reads.

Joint Tenancy

The most common kind of ownership for husbands and wives is Joint Tenancy, in which two (or more) people co-own the property. When one dies, his or her share passes automatically to the other owner(s) without probate.

Although this is the most common type of ownership, it's not necessarily the best for everyone. Here are some of the advantages and disadvantages:

Advantages

1. Because there is no probate on jointly owned property, it is subject to less public exposure than willed property. In addition, it is exempt from probate-related administrative costs.
2. Except for the mortgagee, jointly owned property is free from liens or claims from creditors upon the death of one spouse.

Disadvantages

1. Although jointly owned property may not be subject to the administrative costs of probate, it is usually considered part of the deceased's estate and is therefore taxable.
2. Since jointly owned property passes directly to the surviving co-owner(s), it cannot be placed in a trust, or divided between several heirs. Control rests with the survivor.

Tenancy by the Entirety

This form of ownership is pretty much the same as Joint Tenancy, except that it is limited to husbands and wives and applies only to real estate. It has advantages and disadvantages similar to those of Joint Tenancy.

Tenancy in Common

Each owner has an individual half-interest in the whole property. Each may sell, give away, or leave to heirs his or her interest (though there are serious practical difficulties in effecting such disposition without the cooperation of the other owner).

Community Property

In some states community property laws give each spouse one-half ownership of their combined property regardless of whose name appears as the owner. Community property states include: Arizona, California, Idaho, Louisiana, Nevada, New Mexico, Texas, and Washington.

BUYING A HOUSE

Buying or selling a house is probably the largest legal transaction you'll make. It is possible to manage this transaction by yourself, but it may not be a wise decision. Since many thousands of dollars and your well-being are riding on it, and many complex actions have to be taken, a lawyer's assistance should be well worth the fee. This is especially true when you are considering a condominium, a cooperative, or a move to a retirement community. An attorney will spot the "fine print" and loopholes you may overlook.

Here are some of the steps involved in buying or selling a home.

Selecting a Broker

If you're selling a home, you might want to enlist the services of a broker or real estate agent. Agents will show your home to potential buyers and can charge a fee simply for finding a potential buyer, regardless of whether a sale eventually takes place. If you choose to employ a real estate agent, learn about his or her reputation beforehand—and understand your mutual responsibilities before you sign anything. Also, look into multiple listing services under which several agents will show your home.

Sales Agreement

Once a a buyer is found, the broker will draw up a sales agreement stating the terms of the sale. In addition to stating the agreed-upon price, this agreement should list certain basic understandings, such as grounds for cancellation by either party, accountability for property defects after closing, and grounds for deposit refund should either party wish to withdraw. The agreement should also provide a reasonable time, if needed, for the buyer to obtain a mortgage loan.

Since this document is binding on both parties, it's wise for both the buyer and the seller to get legal counsel before signing. If you are the buyer, beware of agents who try to rush you into signing a sales agreement without legal counsel.

Mortgage Money

Several different kinds of financial institutions provide mortgage money, so shop around. Even slight variations in mortgage rates mean a great deal of money in the long run. Mortgage lending institutions include commercial banks, mutual savings banks, savings and loan associations, mortgage companies, and life insurance companies. In addition, the Veterans' Administration (VA) and the Federal Housing Administration (FHA) guarantee mortgage loans for those who are eligible.

When you choose a mortgage, make sure you understand all the terms of that particular mortgage. Some charge miscellaneous service fees; others have escalating interest rates. A lawyer or financial advisor can help you.

Closing

Closing is a complex and confusing procedure, and a lawyer will make sure your interests are protected throughout.

At the signing of the sales agreement, the buyer's down payment and the sales agreement are placed "in escrow" and held by a third party, such as the real estate company or bank. Lawyers for both the seller and buyer will work with their clients to assure that the terms first agreed upon at the time the down payment was made have been met before closing can take place.

When you buy a home, the lawyer will help determine your rights and responsibilities during the period between the signing of the sales agreement and closing. He or she will conduct a title search (or work with a title-insurance company in conducting a search) to assure that there are no other claims on the property. The lawyer will also examine and advise you regarding the bond you must sign in order to receive the mortgage loan, and advise you on other purchase-related matters, such as homeowners and mortgage insurance.

When you sell a home, your lawyer will figure out how much money is due you for items such as the unused portion of real estate taxes, municipal service payments, and utility payments you have made. If you have chosen to sell a house on your own, it's especially important to have a lawyer to assure you that your interests have been represented.

OTHER LEGAL MATTERS

Starting a Business

If you're thinking of starting a small business (see page 21), either by yourself or with a partner, consult a lawyer in your planning process. He or she can advise you on such matters as registering your business, obtaining a franchise (if needed), adhering to zoning codes, and conforming to other laws.

If you contemplate a partnership, legal assistance in drafting the necessary papers will be important. Don't make the mistake typical of so many who, like John in the introduction to this chapter, had to learn the hard way. A business relationship can wreak havoc on a personal relationship, whether with family members or with friends.

Contracts

A contract is a legally binding agreement. Understanding exactly what you're getting into when you "sign on the dotted line" will save you much trouble, especially if you're making these agreements frequently as part of your retirement plan.

You can help protect yourself against legal and financial tangles by reading any contract carefully before you sign it. Despite what someone might tell you, a standard form contract can be altered. Cross out parts you don't want, initial any such changes yourself, and have all other parties involved in the contract initial them too. If you have any doubts about your obligations, have a lawyer examine the contract before you sign it.

Your signature is your legal identity. Keep track of where you put it! A file of all major documents you sign is a good thing to have.

Power of Attorney

If you can't act on your own behalf in certain legal matters, giving someone your power of attorney will let that person act for you. It's a useful device if you're ill, plan to be away on an extended vacation, or if you cannot conduct your affairs in person for some reason. The signature of the person you choose to represent you becomes *your* legally binding word.

Giving someone your power of attorney is accomplished by having a document prepared and getting it signed by you, your "attorney in law" (the person you're giving your power of attorney to), and a notary public. In this document, you can specify details of the arrangement—which matters the person shall represent you in, and for how long a period of time the agreement is effective.

Conservators or Guardians

If you have a close friend or relative who is incapable of managing his or her own affairs, it may be wise for you (or someone else) to be appointed their conservator or guardian. A conservator acts as a financial caretaker, paying bills, making purchases and investments, arranging affairs, and keeping an accurate financial record. A guardian has full responsibility for a person and/or his or her property. However, the person whose affairs are to be managed by a guardian must be declared incompetent by the court.

The proper documents for both these circumstances should be drafted by a lawyer. Guardianship and conservatorship, as well as power of attorney, terminate upon the death of the one being served.

Divorce and Remarriage

When a marriage breaks up, it is usually under conditions of great emotional stress. Sound judgment can be clouded by anger or guilt. It is especially important, therefore, that persons preparing for a divorce get good legal counseling. Otherwise, bad decisions may be made, or important areas, such as pension contributions and insurance policies, may be overlooked in a settlement.

THE WIZARD OF ID — by Brant parker and Johnny hart

On the other hand, remarriage poses particular legal and financial problems, *and* at this time, too, your judgment may be blurred by emotional concerns. A second marriage is something you may not be contemplating right now. But, you should be aware of the need to assess some of the legal and financial aspects of remarrying before actually doing so.

If you plan to remarry, you may want to reconsider the terms of your present will. Your spouse-to-be is legally entitled to a certain percentage of your estate, unless he or she signs a legally valid prenuptial agreement waiving that entitlement. This kind of agreement can also be made during the marriage. It should be prepared by a lawyer to assure that it will be binding in court.

You should be aware of the legal status of prenuptial agreements in your state before you make one. In any case, discussing your concerns with your intended spouse, and perhaps with your children, may save heartache later on.

Your Rights

Older Americans are protected from discrimination under several federal laws. If you feel that you or someone you know has been discriminated against because of age, sex, or both, you are entitled to legal recourse in these areas:

- Employment—The Age Discrimination in Employment Act prohibits discrimination against persons age forty to seventy who are either looking for work or are already in the work force in both the public and private sectors.
- Credit—The Equal Credit Opportunity Act states that you cannot be denied credit on the basis of sex or marital status (this may be useful to widows or divorcées who are denied credit).

There are also many state laws that apply to these areas and to housing. If you feel you have been the victim of discrimination, you should first go to the person or organization that you believe treated you unfairly. Explain your dissatisfaction to them—perhaps the problem can be resolved there. If not, you can contact an appropriate agency: the U.S. Department of Labor, Equal Opportunity Commission, a local consumer advocacy group or state human rights agency.

In most areas small claims courts are available to handle consumer and other matters. It is not necessary to have an attorney represent you in small claims court. The legal situations in which the average person finds himself are usually not worth "suing" over. But, in cases of money owed, or damage to property or person, in which the dollar amount to settle the case is relatively low,* the small claims court can settle your dispute at a minimal cost and in a reasonable period of time.

The legal world can be complex and confusing. It's important to have professional legal help when you make your retirement plans. Making a will, planning your estate, and buying or selling a home are areas where a lawyer's guidance is vital. Finally, you should know enough about the law and its implications so that you can protect your rights and those of people you care about both now and throughout retirement.

It is important to keep an "inventory and location list" of all papers and documents concerning your home and other properties, insurance policies,

---

*Each state sets a different maximum a small claims court can handle, usually around $500 to $2,500.

bonds, stocks, valuable items and collections, your wills, pension plan, and bank accounts. The location of many of these papers is important and should be known and readily accessible upon the death of one or both of the parties they involve. You lawyer's office, your own fireproof file, a safe deposit box—these are all good places to keep valuable papers. Let others (spouse, relative, close friend) know where these papers are.

THE LIVING WILL*

Advanced technology in the medical field for "combating" death through various life-support systems has created the issue and concern felt by many people over "death with dignity." This whole area of elective death is legally debatable as cases are being tried all over the country.

A LIVING WILL

TO MY FAMILY, MY PHYSICIAN, MY LAWYER, MY CLERGYMAN
TO ANY MEDICAL FACILITY IN WHOSE CARE I HAPPEN TO BE
TO ANY INDIVIDUAL WHO MAY BECOME RESPONSIBLE FOR MY HEALTH, WELFARE, OR AFFAIRS

Death is as much a reality as birth, growth, maturity, and old age—it is the one certainty of life. If the time comes when I, _____, can no longer take part in decisions for my own future, let this statement stand as an expression of my wishes, while I am still of sound mind. If the situation should arise in which there is no reasonable expectation of my recovery from physical or mental disability, I request that I be allowed to die and not be kept alive by artificial means or "heroic measures." I do not fear death itself as much as the indignities of deterioration, dependence, and hopeless pain. I therefore ask that medication be mercifully administered to me to alleviate suffering even though this may hasten the moment of death. This request is made after careful consideration. I hope you who care for me will feel morally bound to follow its mandate. I recognize that this appears to place a heavy responsibility upon you, but it is with the intention of relieving you of such responsibility and of placing it upon myself in accordance with my strong convictions, that this statement is made.

Signed _____

Date _____
Witness _____
Witness _____

Copies of this request have been given to _____
_____
_____
_____

---

*Reprinted with permission of Concern for Dying, 150 West 57th Street, New York, N.Y. 10107

IMPORTANT

Declarants may wish to add specific statements to the Living Will to be inserted in the space provided for that purpose above the signature. Possible additional provisions are suggested below:

1. a) I appoint _____
       to make binding decisions concerning my medical treatment.

                            OR

   b) I have discussed my views as to life-sustaining measures with the following who understand my wishes

       _____ ,
       _____ ,
       _____ .

2. Measures of artificial life support in the face of impending death that are especially abhorrent to me are:
   a) Electrical or mechanical resuscitation of my heart when it has stopped beating.
   b) Nasogastric tube feedings when I am paralyzed and no longer able to swallow.
   c) Mechanical respiration by machine when my brain can no longer sustain my own breathing.
   d) _____

3. If it does not jeopardize the chance of my recovery to a meaningful and sentient life or impose an undue burden on my family, I would like to live out my last days at home rather than in a hospital.

4. If any of my tissues are sound and would be of value as transplants to help other people, I freely give my permission for such donation.

On page 83 is a sample "Living Will" developed by the Euthanasia Education Council. Because this is a very personal and emotional issue, we leave the example to speak for itself and advise anyone considering the making of a living will to seek guidance from their physician, family, and attorney.

SITUATIONS TO CONSIDER

Following are a number of situations that pose problems related to the subject of this chapter. There are no right or wrong "answers" to these situations. They are presented simply to stimulate your thinking about retirement and to emphasize certain aspects of retirement planning. It is not necessary to arrive at any particular conclusion about each case.

It's a good idea for couples to review the situations separately and then share their thoughts. If you are single, perhaps you have a friend, relative, or

THE WIZARD OF ID   by Brant parker and Johnny hart

clergyman with whom you can exchange ideas. Discussing situations like these can help to clarify key aspects of retirement planning and will enable you to become more in tune with your feelings and those of others.

Situation 1: Who Needs a Will?

Clara and Sam own their unmortgaged home and a cabin cottage at a small lake. They have a few savings bonds to meet an emergency. Sam will retire from his government job in two years with a good pension. They have written a long list of instructions in case of their death. A friend tells them to have it notarized. What should they do?

Possible Approaches

1. Do nothing more; as long as the letter is signed, it can act as their will.
2. Have the letter notarized to make it legal.
3. Their estate is so small the letter is good enough.
4. Hire a lawyer to convert the intent of the letter into a will.

Thoughts to Consider

1. Who needs a will?
2. Do you have a valid, updated will?
3. Is a hand-drawn, do-it-yourself will legal? Will having it notarized make it legal? Who can you check with?
4. Should Clara and Sam have separate wills? If so, how often should they be updated?

Situation 2: Entering a Partnership

George's friend retired and opened a bookstore two years ago. The business is growing but it is not making much money. The friend wants George to join him as a partner. George is very interested, but he would have to put up $10,000 to help expand the business. What should George do?

Thoughts to Consider

1. Should George have an accountant take a look at the health of the business?
2. Should George have his attorney help him investigate this business venture and advise him on the proper legal form it should take?
3. What could go wrong if George does not seek legal counsel?

4. Have you ever entered into a financial agreement without consulting an attorney and then been sorry?
5. What would you do if you were George?

Situation 3: How to Choose a Lawyer

John has never had a lawyer. Even when he bought the house, the seller's lawyer handled all legal matters. He has accumulated assets worth nearly $80,000. A magazine article has made him begin to feel as though he should have a lawyer to draft a will and act as a legal advisor. He is wondering how he can find a lawyer, and he's concerned about the expense. How should he do it?

Possible Approaches

1. Check with friends to get suggestions.
2. Use the yellow pages and call several nearby lawyers to ask about services and fees.
3. Check information in local library (several directories of information on lawyers are there).
4. Call the local Bar Association for advice.

Thoughts to Consider

1. Do you have an attorney?
2. What qualities do you want your attorney to have?
3. How can you evaluate the services of an attorney before doing business with him or her? After doing business?
4. Are lawyers' fees negotiable?
5. Are free or reduced-payment legal services available in your community? Who is eligible to receive these services?
6. What should you do if you have problems with an attorney, either yours or someone else's, because of his or her poor practices?

Situation 4: When in Doubt, Don't Sign

Martha had the pleasure of a friendly visit by a young man from Pleasure Heating, Inc. who was inspecting furnaces. He pointed out that she was fortunate not to have had a serious fire—supposedly the fire box was nearly burned through and the dampalator was bad. With relief she signed the "standard form contract" to have $100 worth of parts installed. Later she read the fine print and was dismayed when she saw that the labor charge was $500. What action should she take?

Possible Approaches

1. Ask for a long-term payment plan.
2. Call her lawyer and get advice.
3. Get another company's report and estimate.
4. Tear up the contract and tell Pleasure Heating she has changed her mind.
5. Call the D.A. and prefer charges of fraud and misrepresentation.

Thoughts to Consider

1. Has anyone you know ever been "taken" by a consumer fraud or swindle? Did they report it? How was it resolved?
2. Does this kind of thing happen frequently to older adults who live alone? Why?
3. Where can you go for help if you think you've been taken advantage of?
4. How might you prevent this sort of thing from happening to you?

Situation 5: Dad Needs Help

Lately, Jan has been worried about her father. He seems more and more to be misplacing things. He recently withdrew a large amount of money from his savings account and forgot where he put the cash. Jan feels she should do something, but she doesn't know what. What should Jan do?

Possible Approaches

1. Nothing. Unless her father asks for help, Jan should let him be.
2. Ask her father if something is wrong.
3. Suggest to her father that he see a doctor, quickly.
4. Investigate getting her father's power of attorney.
5. Investigate getting appointed her father's conservator.
6. Investigate getting appointed her father's guardian.

Thoughts to Consider

1. What do you think is a child's responsibility to a parent whose competency is beginning to be doubted?
2. What is the difference between a conservator and a guardian?
3. What kind of assistance does Jan's father need? Medical? Legal? Financial? Other?
4. What if this was your father or mother?
5. How easy is it to take charge in a situation like this? (Should you or could you?)
6. Who might Jan turn to for advice?

REFERENCES AND RESOURCES

Dukeminier, Jesse, and Stanley Johanson. *Family Wealth Transactions: Trusts, Future Interests and Estate Planning* (Supplement to 1978 Ed.). Boston: Little, Brown & Co., 1982.

Dunn, Thomas T. *A Lawyer's Advice to Retirees.* Garden City, N.Y.: Doubleday, 1981.

Kirsch, Charlotte. *A Survivor's Manual to Wills, Trusts, Maintaining Stability.* Garden City, N.Y.: Doubleday, 1981.

Magee, David S. *Everything Your Heirs Need to Know About You.* Aurora, Ill.: Caroline House Publishers, 1982.

Schandel, Terry K. *Tax Tactics for the Singled and Divorced*. New York: Atheneum, 1982.

Soled, Alex J. *The Essential Guide to Wills, Estates, Trusts and Death Taxes*. Baltimore: Chancery Publishers, Inc., 1981.

Your Retirement Legal Guide. Washington, D.C.: American Association of Retired Persons (1909 K St., N.W., 20006).

Chapter 4
If You Are Alone

CHAPTER 4 WARM-UP

Before reading "If You Are Alone," test your knowledge of the subject by placing a check mark next to the answer you prefer. Check the key at the end to find the right answer.

1. Most funerals are arranged after death.   True_____ False_____

2. In general, it's only necessary for one person in a family to understand its financial and legal status.   True_____ False_____

3. Grieving for the loss of a loved one is a natural and healthy reaction.   True_____ False_____

4. Fears and anxieties about being alone can be lessened by talking about them.   True_____ False_____

5. Most women know how and when to provide maintenance and repair on a home or car.   True_____ False_____

6. Generally, in middle age we begin to think more about the possibility of being alone or predeceasing our spouses.   True_____ False_____

7. Few decisions should be made during a time of emotional stress.   True_____ False_____

8. Positive planning can help eliminate our fears of the future.   True_____ False_____

9. Loved ones can often resent us for not "taking better care of ourselves."   True_____ False_____

10. Dying people often feel a strong need to retain control over their medical treatment and personal affairs.   True_____ False_____

Key: 1. (T), 2. (F), 3. (T), 4. (T), 5. (F), 6. (T), 7. (T), 8. (T), 9. (T), 10. (T).

FACING DEATH

No one wants to face death. And no one who does face it can do so easily. But difficult as it is, we need to come to terms with death and to plan for it. Otherwise, we may live out our remaining years in anxiety or may not plan caringly for those whom we will leave behind. But how do we come to terms with death? And what can we do now to help those who will have to carry on without us?

First, it is important that we learn not to run away from thoughts and fears about death, for trying to bury fears within us only intensifies their power over us. It is better to face our fears and to talk about them with others. Some people may respond to talk about dying by saying, "Don't talk that way!" They do this because they themselves are afraid. They fear their own death, or they fear the changes that the death of others would cause in their life. Yet, talking about death can be helpful and important, even though it is discomforting. It gives us an opportunity to deal with hidden emotions, to cope with unnerving fears, to make necessary decisions about the future, and to live our lives wisely and usefully.

For many, middle age is a time when thoughts of death come frequently. The youthful assumption that we will live forever is replaced by the realization that we are all growing older and will eventually die. Fear and anxiety about this are particularly high among the middle aged. Surveys of older adults show, however, that fear of death actually declines as we grow older.

Some people find help in facing death through religious faith. They are able to accept the darkness, because within it a light shines. They are able to accept the waste in life and their failures over the years because they are confident of a forgiveness that is greater than their guilt. Some people find help in the hopes they have for others—for their children and their children's children. Or they are strengthened by the conviction that what they did in life will continue to benefit others long after they have died.

It is important for each of us to find ways to face our death in the context of peace and of caring for those we love. That does not mean that we ever reach the point where we welcome death. Life is too sweet for that! But it does mean that we seek the courage that keeps the fear of death from twisting our life and robbing us of its joy. When we do face death and develop that kind of courage, the possibility is opened to us to live caringly and responsibly.

After we die, some of those who have been near to us will have difficulties in carrying on without us. They are people who depended on us heavily for many things—work around the house, record keeping, entertainment, support, or love. Their life was inextricably tied to ours; it will be hard for them without us. It will be hard for them to establish new patterns and an individual identity, and to overcome the grief and heartache of being alone. We can help to minimize these adjustments while we are alive.

PLANNING YOUR OWN
FUNERAL

Planning your own funeral may sound a little morbid, but it may be one of the most thoughtful and kind steps that you can take on behalf of your loved ones. Most funerals are arranged only after death, when people are too distraught to make plans calmly and wisely. Important decisions are made in too short a time and under great emotional strain. How much better it would be if you were to make these arrangements beforehand and arrange for the other important steps that must be taken in the days and weeks after your death, or after the death of a loved one.

Many people have come to see the value of discussing their funeral and related arrangements with their minister, priest, or rabbi. Together they can plan the kind of service they would want and the family would appreciate.

Freed from having to plan these details with the family after death, the clergyman could spend more time helping the family in its grief. The family, additionally, would feel much better knowing that everything was done as desired.

We can also be helpful to those we love and live with if we increasingly share responsibilities and encourage them to develop skills in areas where we have done everything. We certainly do not want to leave people we care about handicapped in any way because they were kept in the dark, or because too much was done for them and not enough by them.

We should also remember to let those we love know how much their love has meant to us. It is good, on occasion, to take time to reminisce about the joys and satisfactions of the past. When we die, those near to us will naturally feel guilty and sad about many things. It will be important to them to remember that there were many beautiful and rich experiences that were deeply enjoyed and appreciated. And it will be equally important for them to know that you forgave them for what was not so beautiful.

It may be, of course, that we will outlive our husband or wife or our loved ones. In this case, it is important to know how we can most helpfully deal with their dying and how, after they have died, we can focus on a new life for ourselves.

HELPING LOVED ONES WHO ARE DYING

To help people near to us who are dying, we need to have and to show understanding. Particularly, we need to understand how such people feel, and that their feelings change over time. Being with people who are dying is an extremely difficult task. At the same time we must understand what they are going through and we must deal with our own emotions. When we learn that

loved ones are dying we begin to grieve, because we know that they will soon be no longer with us. If we are to provide love and comfort we must go beyond our personal loss and pay careful attention to their needs.

Early in the course of terminal illnesses we may be faced with decisions as to whether or not the ill people should be told of the seriousness of their illness. There is a natural tendency to want to protect them from bad news. Most seriously ill people already know that their situation is grave. Some wish to avoid a frank discussion of the illness, perhaps because they are not ready to deal with its reality or because they don't wish to embarrass or upset others. Careful listeners will often hear clues as to their loved ones' willingness to talk about their condition.

One of the greatest services we can provide terminally ill people is simply to be with them, to be willing to talk with them openly and honestly about their condition if they wish to do so, and to listen to their fears, hopes, anger, and despair. It is important to let dying people know that they are loved and will not be abandoned in their hour of need.

During such times it is helpful to know that people experience wide ranges of emotions. Perhaps the most common reactions among terminally ill people are denial and depression. Even a person who talks as if the illness is understood and accepted may suddenly talk of future plans. This denial of reality may be a way of taking a vacation from the heavy weight of the illness and what it means.

When people fully realize that they will die from their illness, they will frequently be enveloped in depression. Everything will be lost—home, family, possessions, life itself. At times they will want no one to talk to them about how the grandchildren are doing or how anything else is. They will take such talk by us as a sign that we don't understand how horribly serious their situation is. At other times they may want to talk about themselves and us and express some of their sorrow. It is a difficult time for them and a difficult time for us. We may often be at a loss as to what to do or say. But silence is not so bad, and often is very helpful, if, in the silence, people are together who communicate their feelings for each other with held hands and with eyes that show understanding.

Anger is frequently expressed by dying people. The anger may be directed at God, at life, at medical personnel, or perhaps at us. It is natural for them to feel angry. But it will be hard on us, and confusing, if that anger is directed at us. We can be helpful when this happens by not taking things personally, but by patiently listening and caring.

Dying people have a strong need to feel that they continue to have control over medical treatment and personal affairs and are not excluded from daily

B.C. **by johnny hart**

family concerns and decision making. Failure to involve ill people in problems and decisions concerning the family is often done out of a desire to protect them and help them conserve strength. At the same time, however, this contributes to further isolation and increases their feelings of helplessness and loneliness.

We can be most helpful to dying loved ones by being willing to deal honestly with the situation. Many terminally ill people want very badly to talk about the seriousness of their condition with their loved ones, but cannot because their loved ones are not able to face the situation. Such ill people often die lonely, with words unsaid and business unfinished. Many people report, however, that talking openly about the situation helped them become closer than they had ever been before, and the last days and weeks are richer and more full of love than they thought possible.

OUR OWN FEELINGS

Those closest to the dying person may often need someone to talk to. It is difficult to understand and deal with the feelings and actions of someone who is dying, but it will be just as difficult at times to understand and deal with our own feelings as we watch a loved one die—feelings that may range from guilt and anger to despair or panic. Again, they are natural feelings, but we may need help in dealing with them from someone who understands what we are going through.

We Need to Grieve

After someone near to us has died, someone with whom we shared most of our life, we will grieve. People may say to us, "Don't grieve." "It's all right." They are wrong. It is not all right. It is very painful. It hurts as nothing else has ever hurt. Cry! It is all right to cry. It is one way of showing our love when the one who is loved is gone.

We may feel other things besides grief. We may feel guilt for not having done certain things when our husband or wife was alive. We may feel angry at being abandoned and left all alone, at having to be ignorant of where certain things are or what needs to be done. We may feel lost—the old routines and patterns of living are gone. There is no one to eat breakfast with in the morning, and no one to talk to at night. We are at a loss about what to do or where to go. We may feel despair—despair so deep that we want to die. There will also be many painful days, when holidays come, or anniversaries or birthdays. We think back to what was and now is no longer, and we feel terribly down.

. . . AND AFTERWARDS

The months following the death of someone we love are difficult because we have to deal with all kinds of emotions, and without the help of someone with whom we used to share many of our worries and cares. This is a critical time because we are starting out on our own to make a new life for ourselves. We will have to learn new skills, do things we never dreamed of doing, make friends, and find ways to spend our time usefully.

No one can prevent this time in our life from being painful. People can help and will help, however, if we let them. We may need the help of an attorney or a financial counselor for legal and monetary matters. There will be many matters to take care of involving taxes, property, inheritance, Social Security, insurance, and the like. It will cost us some money to get help with such things, but it may cost us more not to. Very soon after the funeral, we will want to take care of these matters: 1) processing the will, 2) freeing bank accounts, 3) changing title on property, car, stock, etc., 4) settling unpaid bills, while keeping accurate and complete records, and 5) filing life insurance claims.

Other affairs that we must take care of but that we need not be concerned with for a while are income taxes, budgeting, seeing that our own will is as we want it, inheritance and estate taxes, and possibly others if there are minor children or dependents. We should keep in close communication with a knowledgeable friend or our attorney to be sure all necessary tasks are accomplished.

During the period after the death of our spouse we may also need the emotional support that counseling by a psychologist or clergyman can give, particularly if we find that our grieving does not lessen after about six weeks. But most of all we need to help ourselves. We need to find the power within ourselves to start a new life and to begin to discover who we are, what our potentials are, and what possibilities lie before us.

The future is ours. It will not be easy, but we can make it.

BEING ALONE

If you have spent most of your life as a single person—unmarried, widowed, or divorced—you've had to learn to act on your own initiative; make important decisions without relying on others; and do almost everything for yourself. However, if you've been married, you have grown accustomed to relying on your spouse to help you make certain decisions and plans. You have had many things done for you that single people have to do for themselves. In many ways your life has revolved around your role as a wife or husband.

What will happen if, after spending your adult years in partnership with another, you must suddenly begin to face life alone? Thinking about or suddenly becoming alone is difficult and discomforting. But also disturbing is the thought of entering single life completely unprepared to make decisions and to handle necessary day-to-day affairs.

Even if you've never been married, chances are that your life is closely intertwined with another person's—a close friend, sister, or brother. Loss of the closeness and support provided by that person will also require a major adjustment.

Being Prepared

How can anyone be prepared for being a widow or widower?

It may not be possible to be ready completely for the shock of learning that your spouse is dying or has died. One thing you can do in this regard is to try to understand the emotions you are feeling. Remember—it's normal to grieve! Grief is the way our minds and hearts become reconciled to giving up a loved one.

There are other ways to prepare, however, and they have to do with the practical aspects of life.

Too many times a woman discovers after the death of her husband that, in addition to her loneliness and grief, she must deal with such things as money management, insurance, and maintenance and repair of a home. These are the things that were considered her husband's responsibility when he was alive and with which she has never concerned herself.

If your spouse should die, would you have sufficient income? Would you have adequate health insurance? Do you know where all your valuable papers are? Can you perform the regular routines of the house? Can you manage your own financial affairs?

In the old days, it was considered strictly the man's responsibility to manage the financial affairs of the family. Those days are gone. In fact, women nowadays sometimes handle all the financial affairs. Ideally, financial plans and major decisions regarding finances should be made jointly. Each partner should be fully capable of handling the joint financial affairs.

WHEN YOU ARE ALONE

Up to this point, we have been talking about preparing for death in regard to practical matters and the feelings of a dying person and the spouse of the dying person. We have also dealt with the emotions one feels when a partner dies and the importance of allowing oneself to grieve for the loss of the loved one.

Eventually, however, through the grief comes the realization that you are alone and must now build a new life, a new identity. You may enter this period with a feeling of loneliness and apprehension. You ask yourself: who are your friends? How will you use your time so as to avoid loneliness and boredom? What should be done with the house? The children have invited you to live with them—should you accept? What is your financial situation? Should you consider the possibility of remarriage? These and many more questions may come to mind.

The important thing to remember, however, is that you can handle the changes that lie ahead if you think clearly, don't make rash decisions, and take one step at a time. If you maintain the conviction that you can build a new life, you can become an independent person.

Where Should You Live?

One of the first decisions you may face is in regard to where you should live. You may be asked to make this decision sooner than you think. A natural reaction for your children might be to invite you to live with them soon after your spouse's death. In your grief and loneliness this may sound like a tempting offer, but you should give it careful consideration before making a decision.

If you have a child living nearby it may be a good idea to accept such an offer—for a few weeks. The emotional support may be very helpful. You shouldn't make any permanent decisions, however, until after you have moved back to your own home and have carefully examined each of your options. This isn't just an economic decision. You must face the basic problem of your fear of being alone and balance it against your need to feel independent and self-reliant.

Should You Seek Employment?

If you have been employed for most or all of your married life, it may not seem strange to contemplate continuing or seeking employment after the loss of your spouse. But if you have not worked for a living recently because your time was occupied with raising a family or because you have been retired for some time, it may come as something of a shock to find that you need to entertain the idea of returning to the work force. Keep in mind that until social attitudes improve toward employing older workers, your opportunities for work may be very limited. But don't hesitate to use your imagination and be aggressive.

The advantages and disadvantages of employment depend almost entirely on the situation that develops after the loss of your partner. There are some obvious advantages. Working provides more income and brings you in contact with other people, combating loneliness. It brings you into contact with new ideas and offers challenges that would not otherwise be available. Work can be a source of personal satisfaction and security—knowing that you are capable and that you are needed and valued as a worker and as a person.

There can be disadvantages to working as well, however. The time and energy required by your employment may leave little for the development of other interests. Tension and anxiety brought on by job pressures could take their toll on your health and happiness.

You must decide for yourself whether employment is the right course of action for you. Refer to the section on employment in the text of "Opportunities and Adjustments" for more on this subject.

Should You Do Volunteer Work?

Volunteer work has provided a tremendous amount of companionship and satisfaction for many bereaved persons over the years. Most communities have organizations specifically set up to coordinate volunteer work. In addition, some communities have an agency known as R.S.V.P. (Retired Senior Volunteer Program) that is concerned exclusively with coordinating the volunteer work of retired people.

How About Travel?

If you have the money and the inclination, travel can be interesting and rewarding—especially if done with friends or as part of a group or club. Don't make the mistake, however, of thinking that by "getting away from it all" your

grief or loneliness will be lessened. These problems must be dealt with directly and solutions must be found that are permanent and satisfactory. If you go on a trip to escape the loneliness and sadness associated with your home and all its memories, the chances are those things will still be there to greet you when you return.

What About Remarriage?

The subject of remarriage may seem foreign to you now. You may not be able or may not want to imagine a situation where you would want to remarry. But when someone's partner dies, the need for love, security, affection, and a mature sexual relationship doesn't disappear. We maintain our need for some or all of these things throughout our lives, even into very old age.

Some widows and widowers hesitate to consider the possibility of remarriage because of a lingering faithfulness to their departed partner. The thought of remarriage makes them feel guilty, so they consciously (or unconsciously) deny that they continue to need a close relationship with another person. But there is no need to feel guilty about remarriage. It would be a tribute to your partner's ability to fulfill your need for love, affection, and security if you should miss those qualities after your partner's death to the extent that you seek them from another.

If, after your partner dies or you are divorced, you become receptive to the idea of remarriage, you may be faced with some perplexing questions about how to meet potential partners and how you should act. You may also find it difficult to find someone who measures up to your idealized memory of your deceased spouse. In addition, your children, even though they are adults, might not like the idea of your remarrying. Part of their lack of enthusiasm might be due to worry that, should you die before your second spouse, a large part of the estate amassed by you and your previous spouse could go to your second spouse and his or her family. In fact, you may have worried about this yourself.

Remarriage is not for everyone. Some find themselves reluctant to give up the sense of independence and self-reliance they developed after the loss of their spouse. Others simply cannot find a suitable partner. Whatever your inclinations, you should try to be open and receptive to changes in your life-style. Regardless of whether you remarry or remain single, you will inevitably shift gradually to a new identity.

The thoughts presented here are to help you find direction at a difficult time in your life. By no means do they cover all you need to know about the subject. Nor will reading by itself prepare you completely. But perhaps they will assist you to begin to prepare yourself in both practical and emotional ways.

SITUATIONS TO CONSIDER

Following are a number of situations that pose problems related to the subject of this chapter. There are no right or wrong "answers" to these situations. They are presented simply to stimulate your thinking about retirement and to emphasize certain aspects of retirement planning. It is not necessary to arrive at any particular conclusion about each case.

It's a good idea for couples to review the situations separately and then share their thoughts. If you are single, perhaps you have a friend, relative, or clergyman with whom you can exchange ideas. Discussing situations like these can help to clarify key aspects of retirement planning and will enable you to become more in tune with your feelings and those of others.

Situation 1: She Wants to Have a Fling

Kris, a recent widow, had an unhappy marriage. She has been left a sizable estate, and feels that she wants to discard the stay-at-home role she has always known and have a fling. A few tours, Las Vegas, Latin America, who knows. After that she wants to be active in her community and cultivate new friends. What should Kris do?

Possible Approaches
1. Have the fling—throw caution to the winds.
2. Go ahead—but don't go alone.
3. Forget it—get into community work, and start making new friends.
4. Think it over for a year—she is overreacting. Besides, people will talk.

Thoughts to Consider
1. Have you ever wanted to go on a wild fling?
2. Is it a good idea to travel alone? Why or why not?
3. Should Kris be concerned with what her family and friends might think?
4. Can we make dramatic changes in our life without going through a period of discomfort or unhappiness with ourselves?
5. Are you able to indulge yourself when others don't understand?

Situation 2: "Come Live With Us"

Mary is deep in grief. Her husband just died unexpectedly at the age of 61. They lived in a big, comfortable house in an older section of town that contains a lot of memories from the early days of their marriage. Right after the funeral Mary's son stated firmly that she was to come live with him and his wife and children. They live in a bigger city about fifty miles away. Mary loves her son and his family but is not sure it's a good idea to do as he advises. What should Mary do?

Possible Approaches

1. Move in with her son but only for a few weeks until she feels better.
2. Don't make any sudden decisions. Stay at home until she has a chance to think it through.
3. Think it through with a close friend or her clergyman.
4. Sell the house and move in with her son to avoid loneliness.
5. Invite a good friend to stay with her for a while.

Thoughts to Consider

1. What are the positive and negative aspects of living with your adult children?
2. Can sympathetic friends or relatives "help" you work through your grief?
3. How wise is it to make important, long-term decisions in a time of emotional stress?
4. Have you ever thought about how you might act in a similar situation? Either as the child of a recent widow/widower or in widowhood?

Situation 3: Single Again!

After twenty-eight years and three children, Hope was suddenly divorced four months ago. A younger woman was involved. Hope was calm at the time. Both family and friends were impressed with how well she handled the change. They are beginning to wonder now, however. She has been acting strangely lately—acts nervous, talks incessantly, repeats herself often, and makes middle-of-the-night phone calls just for small talk. What is wrong, and what should she do about it?

Thoughts to Consider

1. Do you think there is a natural "grieving" process associated with separation and divorce?
2. How are the divorce and the death of a spouse similar? How are they different?
3. How would you react to Hope if you were her friend?
4. Do we sometimes bury our feelings, only to have them surface again later—perhaps at inappropriate times? Why? How can we avoid this?

Situation 4: Husband #2?

Edith's husband Harold died at the relatively early age of fifty-six. That was a year and half ago and now Edith, fifty-five, has met and become engaged to another man. Several times while he was alive Harold mentioned that if he were to die before Edith, he wouldn't want her to remarry and turn over their "fortune" to another man. It's not really a fortune, but Edith wants to comply with his wishes and will their assets to the children. She doesn't want to enter her new relationship with no assets, however. What should she do?

Possible Approaches

1. Give a large portion of the assets to the children while she is alive.
2. Explain what she wants to her fiancé and trust him to comply if she should predecease him.
3. Ask her attorney to draw up a prenuptial agreement stating her wishes.
4. Have a new will drawn up stating how she wants her assets distributed.

Thoughts to Consider

1. Do you think Edith's situation is fairly common?
2. What about the feelings of the new husband? His children?
3. How strongly are we influenced by our past?
4. Who can help Edith with her problem? An attorney? Her children?
5. What would you do if you were entering a new marriage after the death of a spouse.

Situation 5: Good Grief?

George has been having a very difficult time since his wife Judith's death four months ago. Her death was unexpected and George had to take care of all the funeral arrangements. Now, he seems melancholy all the time. He can't sleep well at night and has little appetite. He almost always feels tired and listless. His friends say he isn't being fair to himself or Judith's memory. They're also beginning to worry because this has been going on since the funeral. What should they do?

Possible Approaches

1. Leave George alone. He'll come out of his grief in his own time.
2. Urge him to see a doctor. He isn't getting enough rest, and he isn't eating properly so he's probably undernourished.
3. Try to get him to talk about his feelings.
4. Convince him to see a psychologist or other counselor.
5. Try to include him in more social activities.

Thoughts to Consider

1. Do you believe there are limits to a normal, healthy grieving period? How long would you consider "normal"?
2. Does everyone grieve in the same way? What are some of the ways we grieve? How have you grieved over a loss?
3. Do you think it would have helped George if Judith had preplanned her own funeral? Do you think preplanning your funeral is a good idea? If you had the opportunity to plan yours, what would it be like?

4. Do people sometimes do odd things or behave strangely "in remembrance" of a loved one? How would you like your family to remember you?
5. Would it do any good for George to talk to someone about how he is feeling?
6. What would you do if you were George's friend?

REFERENCES AND RESOURCES

A Guide Book for Widows, and for Those Called Upon to Aid Widows. Hartford, Conn.: Life Insurance Agency Management Association (170 Sigourney St., 06105).

Fisher, Ida, and Byron Lane. *The Widow's Guide: How to Adjust—How to Grow.* New York: Prentice-Hall, 1981.

Harvey, Carol D. and Howard M. Bahr. *The Sunshine Widows: Adapting to Sudden Bereavement.* Lexington, Mass.: Lexington Books, 1980.

Kahn, Lawrence E. *When Couples Part: How the Legal System Can Work for You.* New York: Franklin-Watts, 1981.

Kubler-Ross, Elizabeth. *Living with Death and Dying.* New York: Macmillan, 1981.

Kurtz, Eleanor. *What a Widow Needs to Know: A Guide for Widows and Helpers.* Palo Alto: R & E Research Associates, 1982.

Kushner, Harold S. *When Bad Things Happen to Good People.* New York: Schocken, 1981.

Loewinsohn, Ruth Jean. *Survival Handbook for Widows.* Chicago: Follett Publishing Co., 1979.

Lukeman, Brenda. *Embarkations: A Guide to Dealing with Death and Parting.* Englewood Cliffs, N.J.: Prentice-Hall, 1982.

Payne, Dorothy. *Life After Divorce.* New York: Pilgrim Press, 1982.

Riley, Miles O. *Set Your House in Order: A Practical Way to Prepare for Death.* Garden City, N.Y.: Doubleday, 1980.

Rosenberg, Jay F. *Thinking Clearly About Death.* Englewood Cliffs, N.J.: Prentice-Hall, 1983.

Stoddard, Sandol. *The Hospice Movement: A Better Way of Caring for the Dying.* Briarcliff Manor, N.Y.: Stein & Day, 1978.

Vail, Elaine. *A Personal Guide to Living with Loss.* New York: John Wiley & Sons, Inc., 1982.

Chapter 5
Income Planning

CHAPTER 5 WARM-UP

Before reading "Income Planning," test your knowledge of the subject by placing a check mark next to the answer you prefer. Check the key at the end to find the correct answer.

1. It's never too early or too late to work on establishing a retirement estate.   True_____ False_____

2. You don't have to pay income taxes on earnings you contribute to an Individual Retirement Account (IRA).   True_____ False_____

3. A good way to build a retirement nest egg is through a whole life insurance policy.   True_____ False_____

4. The earliest you can collect retirement benefits from Social Security is: 50___ 55___ 62___ 65___

5. Your Social Security benefit will be based on your five best years of wages.   True_____ False_____

6. Social Security retirement benefits go up each year to help retirees keep up with inflation.   True_____ False_____

7. As a retiree, you can earn as much as you wish in wages or salary without losing Social Security benefits.   True_____ False_____

8. Medicare is not the only health insurance you will need in retirement.   True_____ False_____

9. All pension plans provide for full vesting after ten years.   True_____ False_____

10. It's a good idea to have a professional financial advisor periodically review your investment plans.   True_____ False_____

11. A married woman who has worked under Social Security can collect her own benefit or a percentage of her husband's benefit, whichever is higher.   True_____ False_____

Key: 1. (T), 2. (T), 3. (F), 4. (62), 5. (F), 6. (T), 7. (F), 8. (T), 9. (F), 10. (T), 11. (T).

INCOME PLANNING

"After I retire, how much money will I have coming in and where will it come from?" These questions are probably uppermost in the minds of those contemplating retirement. Another important and frequently asked question is, "How much income will I need in retirement?" It's impossible to say with certainty what future costs of living will be, but one thing you must count on is that inflation, unfortunately, is going to be with us for quite some time. You must plan to live with it. This makes it more important than ever that you take a close look at your present financial situation, what you expect it to be when you retire, and what it might be several years after retirement. For some, this might raise another question, "What can I do to increase my retirement income?"

The uncertainty of the future cannot be eliminated even by careful planning, but you can significantly improve your chances for a financially secure retirement. More than ever before, the decisions you make and the actions you take now will have a strong bearing on your financial status in retirement. Naturally, the more time you have to prepare for retirement, the better your chances of building a solid financial future. But even if retirement is in your near future, the choices you make now can strongly affect your retirement income.

In this chapter we will discuss the sources from which you will draw your retirement income, including your personal investments, Social Security, and your pension plan. Other important financial topics will also be examined, such as life insurance, early retirement, Medicare, and even starting a new business. Although this chapter is not intended to give you all the information you need to financially plan your retirement, it will provide you with important basic information to begin with.

Here are some critically important ideas for you to keep in mind as you read the material:

1. *Establish financial goals*—You must determine where you want to be financially when you retire before you can devise a plan to get there. To do this you will need to consider how much money you will require to live on in retirement, where that money will come from, and what you can afford to contribute in the coming years toward your retirement fund. Doing this will at the same time help you clarify your present spending priorities.
2. *Seek professional advice*—Even if your means are quite moderate, the ability to squeeze as much as possible out of your assets can make a significant difference. In most instances the fees you pay for advice are easily paid back by higher rates of return and lower taxes.
3. *Develop a positive attitude toward your retirement finances*—Don't get the feeling that there is nothing much you can do, or that everything is just too complicated, because it is simply not true. You can affect your retirement financial condition if you firmly decide to take action and invest some of your time in thinking about your future. Inflation cannot be eliminated by ignoring it. You must, and you can, learn to live with it.
4. *If you have not already done so, start now on a financial plan for retirement*—don't just rely on Social Security and your pension because it won't be enough. A major part of your retirement income must come from your personal investments, and the sooner you begin, the better off you will be.

PLANNING TOOLS

How Much Money Will You Need in Retirement?

When you retire, whether it be next year or fifteen years from now, how much money will you need to live comfortably? This is difficult to answer because there are several key factors that you can only estimate, such as the rate of inflation between now and your retirement, and changes in your daily living expenses. Nevertheless, this can be a valuable exercise because it gives you a clearer picture of where you want to be financially when you retire and what you need to accomplish in the way of personal financial planning.

Use these three steps to estimate how much income you will need from all sources to enable you to maintain your standard of living.

Step 1. Estimate your replacement rate.

        If you retired today, what percentage of your immediate preretirement income would you need in order to maintain your standard of living? Financial planners advise that you shoot for 65–75% replacement.

Present Net Income	_____
Replacement Rate	×_____
Retirement Income Needed Today	$_____

Step 2. Estimate the numbers of years to your retirement and the average inflation rate you expect until then. Locate the inter-section of these num-bers on the chart below.

Years to Retirement	_____
Inflation Rate Expected	_____

Step 3. Multiply the number found in Step 2 by the Retirement Income Today figure found in Step 1. This is the amount of retirement income you will need to keep the same purchas-ing power as you would have if you retired today.

Number of Future Dollars Needed to Equal $1 Today	_____
Retirement Income Today (Step 1)	×_____
Retirement Income You Will Need When You Retire	$_____

Number of Future Dollars Needed to Equal $1 Today

Years to Retirement	Inflation Rate You Expect				
	6%	8%	10%	12%	14%
1	1.06	1.08	1.10	1.12	1.14
2	1.12	1.17	1.21	1.25	1.30
3	1.19	1.26	1.33	1.40	1.48
4	1.26	1.36	1.46	1.57	1.69
5	1.33	1.47	1.61	1.76	1.93
6	1.41	1.59	1.77	1.97	2.19
7	1.49	1.72	1.95	2.21	2.50
8	1.58	1.85	2.14	2.48	2.85
9	1.67	2.00	2.36	2.77	3.25
10	1.78	2.16	2.59	3.11	3.71
11	1.88	2.34	2.85	3.48	4.23
12	2.11	2.52	3.14	3.90	4.82
13	2.23	2.72	3.45	4.36	5.49
14	2.37	2.94	3.80	4.89	6.26
15	2.51	3.18	4.18	5.47	7.13

Know Your Net Worth

Assets Inventory

Assets (Real Estate, Stocks, Bonds, etc.)	Company	Original Purchase Price	Current Value	Rate of Return (avg.)	Reason for Keeping	Could Convert To
_____	_____	_____	_____	_____	_____	_____
_____	_____	_____	_____	_____	_____	_____
_____	_____	_____	_____	_____	_____	_____
_____	_____	_____	_____	_____	_____	_____
_____	_____	_____	_____	_____	_____	_____
_____	_____	_____	_____	_____	_____	_____
_____	_____	_____	_____	_____	_____	_____
_____	_____	_____	_____	_____	_____	_____

Life Insurance and Annuities

Face Value of Policy	Company	Type of Policy	Annual Premium	Current Cash Value	Loans Outstanding	Could Convert To
_____	_____	_____	_____	_____	_____	_____
_____	_____	_____	_____	_____	_____	_____
_____	_____	_____	_____	_____	_____	_____
_____	_____	_____	_____	_____	_____	_____
_____	_____	_____	_____	_____	_____	_____
_____	_____	_____	_____	_____	_____	_____
_____	_____	_____	_____	_____	_____	_____
_____	_____	_____	_____	_____	_____	_____

ASSETS

Liquid Assets
Checking and Savings Accounts _____
Savings Certificates _____
U.S. Savings Bonds _____
U.S. Treasury Bills _____
Money Market Funds _____
Life Insurance Cash Value _____
Other _____

Real Estate (Market Value)
Residence _____
Other Properties _____

Long Term Assets
Stocks (market value) _____
Bonds (market value) _____
Business Equity _____
Pension Accounts _____
Profit Sharing Plan _____
Individual Retirement Account _____
Keogh Plans _____
Annuities _____
Tax Shelters _____
Loans to Others _____

Personal Property
Automobiles _____
Household Goods _____
Jewelry and Furs _____
Other _____

TOTAL ASSETS _____

LIABILITIES

Real Estate
Residence Mortgage _____
Other Mortgages _____

Personal Liabilities
Automobile Loan _____
Credit Card Bills _____
Rent/Taxes _____
Household Accounts _____
Loans _____
Utilities _____
Miscellaneous _____

TOTAL LIABILITIES _____

Total Assets _____
Total Liabilities (—) _____
NET WORTH _____

BUILDING YOUR RETIREMENT ESTATE

Financial planners often speak of the three-legged stool as symbolic of the three basic sources of income in retirement: Social Security, pension, and personal savings. This third leg of the stool has taken on greater importance in recent years as inflation erodes the spending power of pension income and Social Security gradually moves away from being the major source of retirement income.

While the dire predictions about the collapse of Social Security are for the most part unfounded, it is true that the system will be a less important source of income for many future retirees than it has been in the past. This makes it all the more important that your personal retirement estate work as hard as it can at growing, so it will be sufficient for you when you retire.

Importance of Disciplined Savings

Anyone who has faced a financial crisis and had a cushion to fall back on in the form of a savings account will tell you about the importance of disciplined savings. The way to build a nest egg is to faithfully deposit, over a period of years, a portion of your income into an interest-bearing account.

However, the financial world has changed radically in recent years: Laws and regulations have been changed; interest rates on loans and investments have soared; new kinds of investments have been offered. Never before has the individual "small investor" had the range of investment choices available today. No longer can you afford to put your savings in a low-yield passbook savings account. Not only will this money not grow, but it will actually *shrink* in purchasing power: Inflation promises to outstrip the passbook account's ability to keep up. In today's world you have to know what investments you can make that will enable your nest egg to grow as fast as possible while at the same time minimizing your risk. You have to know how you can minimize your tax liability on both your earned income and your investment income. You have to be able to detect where you have "lazy dollars" or money that is not working as hard as it can for you.

With recent changes in federal regulations, the distinctions between financial institutions are fading. Financial experts predict that in the near future there will be financial "supermarkets" offering services that are now available only by working through several separate institutions. The financial institution of the future will offer one-stop shopping for savings, checking, insurance, IRAs, stocks, bonds, and other forms of investment.

SHOULD YOU START AN IRA?

The 1981 Economic Recovery Tax Act allows all working Americans under the age of 70½ to establish an Individual Retirement Account (IRA). This allows you to make tax-deductible contributions to your own retirement plan and earn tax-deferred income, regardless of whether you are covered by another pension plan.

An IRA is simply a personal retirement plan in which you decide when you want your money invested and how much, within limits, you want to contribute annually. IRAs are easy to set up through banks, savings and loan associations, credit unions, brokerage firms, mutual funds, or insurance companies.

In most cases you can set up your IRA with your choice of stocks, bonds, annuities, mutual funds, money market funds, or other traditional investments. Investments that cannot be included in an IRA are collectables such as precious metals, antiques, maps, stamps, works of art, or other tangible personal property as defined by the IRS. As with any investment, you'll want to make sure that you get complete information ahead of time, make up your mind what your investment goals are, and read the fine print.

The beauty of an IRA is that it offers several important tax advantages. The first is that you don't pay income taxes on contributions you make to your account. You can tax deduct all contributions whether or not you itemize your other deductions on your income tax return. This reduces your federal income tax and, in most cases, state taxes as well. If, for example, you are in the 30 percent tax bracket, a $2,000 IRA contribution would save you $600 in income taxes.

The second tax benefit is that earnings from your IRA investments are tax deferred. You pay no income tax on these earnings until you begin to draw from your account in retirement, when you will probably be in a lower tax bracket. This enables your assets to grow faster than if you paid taxes on the earnings each year.

You can contribute any amount up to $2,000 a year to an IRA plan, as long as you earn that much. If your income is less than $2,000 because you only work part-time, you can contribute 100 percent of your income. And you don't have to contribute to your account every year. If you want to vary your contributions from year to year, or skip a year, or several, you are free to do so. If both you and your spouse work, you can each contribute up to $2,000 per year. If only one of you works, a total of $2,250 can be contributed to a joint account.

Be sure when you set up your IRA that you fully intend to leave that money untouched until you retire. The IRS allows these tax advantages with the intention of helping you make your retirement financially secure, and you will pay dearly if you withdraw early. Withdrawals from IRAs cannot be made before age 59½ without a significant tax penalty unless you become certifiably disabled. And, at the latest, you must begin to make withdrawals in the tax year you reach the age of 70½. There are more detailed regulations governing contributions and withdrawals which you should find out about from the financial institution in which you establish your account.

Despite the advertising claims of some financial institutions, IRAs will not create "millionaires" except on paper. An IRA investor who contributes $2,000 per year for 30 years at an average rate of return of 15% will indeed have very close to a million dollars, but in terms of purchasing power of those dollars, that money will be worth far less, because whenever interest rates remain high the inflation rate also remains high.

A more valid way of projecting the true value of an IRA accumulation is to employ what economists refer to as the "real" interest rate, which is the interest rate earned after inflation is taken into account. Over a long period of time the real interest rate has averaged about 3% after subtracting for inflation. This means that, on average, interest rates have been running about 3 percentage points higher than inflation. Using this rate, and assuming a $2,000 IRA contribution each year for 30 years, the account would be worth the equivalent of about $98,000 in today's money.

YOU ARE AN INVESTOR

Are you an investor? If you have a bank account you are. If you own your own home you are. If you own any stocks, bonds, straight or whole life insurance, antiques, gold, diamonds, or almost any form of equity you are indeed an investor.

For any investment you make, whether large or small, there are three major questions you should ask yourself. The answers to these questions will go a long way toward determining whether a particular investment is right for you, and toward determining your overall investment strategy.

The three main questions are:

1. What rate of return do you want or need to make on the investment?
2. How great is the risk of making this investment?
3. How liquid is the investment?

The first two questions are closely related, as there is usually a tradeoff between risk and rate of return. The higher the risk, the greater are the rewards if the investment pays off. But risk means there is always the chance that the investment will pay off poorly, or even that your original investment will decline in value. Speculative stocks, for example, are purchased because the investor is willing to forgo a modest but guaranteed rate of return, seeking instead to take a greater risk in exchange for the chance to earn a significantly higher rate of return. The safest investments are usually government bonds and notes, as they are guaranteed by the Federal Treasury, and bank savings accounts, which are now protected by the Federal Deposit Insurance Corporation (FDIC) up to $100,000.

Interest rates are sometimes directly related to liquidity, that is, how easily the investment can be converted to cash. Bank certificates of deposit, for example, pay higher rates of interest than regular savings accounts, but you have to agree not to withdraw the money for a certain period of time, sometimes several years, in order to obtain the higher rate. Real estate is considered to be among the least liquid forms of investment, because the time required to convert it to cash is usually quite lengthy. Later on in this chapter we will discuss some of the important factors involved in considering an investment in real estate.

The question of liquidity is an important one because it determines how quickly you can get your capital in an emergency or if you want to change investments. Access to and control of your investments are especially important because in recent years interest rates have fluctuated wildly. Several years ago, for example, many people invested in long-term bank certificates of deposit offering, at that time, the attractive interest rate of 8.5 percent. Soon thereafter interest rates went through the ceiling and these investors had to choose between holding on to their low-yielding certificates for many more months, or cashing them in with significant penalties for early withdrawal, so they could reinvest the money at current market rates.

THE WIZARD OF ID   by Brant parker and Johnny hart

WHAT ARE YOUR INVESTMENT OPTIONS?

Passbook Savings Accounts

Passbook accounts have complete flexibility; your money is always immediately available, and you may deposit or withdraw at any time. The trouble with passbook accounts is that interest rates are the lowest among the major types of accounts. The accounts are federally or state insured.

Financial advisors seldom recommend a passbook account because some other possibilities, such as money market accounts, provide a much higher rate of return, are liquid, and are safe.

Certificates of Deposit

Certificates of deposit are good savings plans for those with $500 to $100,000 to invest. Interest rates are the highest paid on any savings account and are based upon the amount deposited and the length of time to maturity (from ninety days to six years). Notice of withdrawal is required and a substantial penalty is imposed for early withdrawal.

Money Market Funds

During the mid 1970's a new opportunity, called money market funds, became available for the smaller, individual investor. Before that time high yields were available only to large investors on $100,000 certificates of deposit. Some of the mutual fund managements decided to establish money market funds so that investors with as little as $1,000 could take advantage of the higher rates by pooling their money with others in the fund. Over the past several years money market funds have grown in popularity because they enable the small investor to earn high short-term interest rates without having to tie up the money for a fixed period of time. There are no commissions on deposits or withdrawals from your money market fund, and you may be able to write checks on the account as well. Because of competition for money market funds some companies now require no minimum deposit either to start or to increase your account.

The yield on money market funds may vary from day to day. Your funds are invested by the brokerage firm in a variety of short-term bank certificates of deposit and government securities. Financial planners usually recommend

that you invest your cash reserves in a money market fund because it is so easily accessible.

Late in 1982 a change in federal banking regulations allowed banks to begin offering accounts with essentially the same features as traditional money market accounts offered by brokerage firms. These new accounts enable banks to pay the same interest rates as other money market funds, with the added bonus of $100,000 in FDIC insurance protection. There are no early withdrawal penalties because you are not committing your money for any specified time period, but there is a $2,500 minimum balance required. If your account falls below that amount you then earn the bank's passbook interest rate. Like mutual fund money market accounts, these have the attractive feature of immediate access and allow you to write a limited number of checks on the account. Some other factors to consider, such as automatic transfers, service charges, detailed statements, and lines of credit, may vary from bank to bank.

Early in 1983 many banks also began to make available regular checking accounts that pay interest at a rate a few percentage points lower than money market rates.

What About Stocks . . .

There are two basic categories of stocks issued by a corporation: common and preferred. Both represent ownership of a portion of the assets of the corporation. Dividends paid on common stock are determined by the board of directors of the corporation. The value of the stock on the market generally fluctuates with confidence in the anticipated earnings of the company and overall economic conditions. There are two ways that a stock can provide a return to the investor. One is through an increase in the trading price of the stock on the stock market, known as capital appreciation or growth. The other is through dividends paid by the company. Some stocks are known for their modest or negligible increase in trading value, and the steady, healthy dividend they pay. These are known as income stocks because they provide the investor with a steady but not spectacular source of income. Other stocks pay little in the way of dividends, instead showing sharper increases in the value of the stock. These are known as growth stocks and are considered to be a somewhat more risky investment, but with potential for more of an increase in the value of the investment.

Most stocks are neither purely income nor purely growth oriented but fall somewhere in between. To a large extent the emphasis is determined by decisions of the management of the corporation about what to do with profits. They can choose to distribute a greater share of the profits to shareholders in the form of dividends or they can plow back most of the profits into the company in order to expand its size in hopes of greater profitability in the future.

Preferred stock carries a fixed dividend rate that must be paid to the owner before dividends are distributed to common-stock holders. To make preferred stock more attractive there may be a convertibility clause offered which says that after a certain date the preferred stock may be converted into common stocks. Thus the fixed dividend preferred stock guarantees an income and gives the investor the opportunity to convert to common stock if the company becomes a big moneymaker.

Financial planners generally advise that the younger you are the more you should stress growth investments, with the stress coming on income-producing investments after retirement, when your need for income from investments is greater and your tax liability is lower. You should keep in mind, however, that even though you may want the income from your investments when you retire, your retirement may cover fifteen to twenty years or longer. It may be wise, then, to retain some growth potential.

. . . And Bonds

A corporate bond represents a loan to the company by the bondholder and indicates that the company promises to pay the holder a fixed rate of interest for a specified period of time. Should the company's assets be liquidated, the bondholders would be the first to be paid.

Bonds can be purchased or sold on the bond market, where the selling price will vary according to the interest rate, the economic health of the company, the value of alternative forms of investment, and general economic conditions.

Municipal Bonds

The bonds of cities, states, and other taxing districts are known as municipal bonds. The attraction of these is that the owner does not have to pay federal, and sometimes state, income tax on the interest. The interest rate on these bonds is usually lower than corporate bonds, but for people in the higher income tax brackets they can provide an attractive alternative. Another kind of municipal bond is known as the pollution bond or industrial revenue bond. These are granted tax exempt status by the municipality but future payment of principal and interest is guaranteed by the company for which they are issued and not by the municipality.

United States Savings Bonds

U.S. savings bonds are guaranteed by the federal government. Treasury notes and savings bonds are among the safest forms of investments available. You can invest in Series EE savings bonds throughout your life, deferring taxes on the interest until you cash them in. If you prefer, you can convert your eligible Series E bonds, savings notes (freedom shares), or Series EE bonds to current income Series HH bonds without paying income taxes on the accrued interest.*

---

*EE and HH bonds are new alternatives for the old E and H bonds. HH bonds are interest deferred until maturity. EE bonds are taxable and are often used as investments for children.

The HH bonds will then pay you interest by treasury check every six months, currently at a level of 7.5 percent per year. Interest earned on HH bonds must be reported each year on your federal income tax return.

Those who currently hold Series E bonds should be aware that interest will no longer be earned on these bonds after they reach final maturity (forty years from date of purchase) and should be cashed in or converted to Series HH bonds in order to avoid loss of interest.

In recent years, with high market-interest rates, savings bonds have been a poor investment because they earned too small a rate of return. To remedy this, on November 1, 1982, the Treasury Department put into effect a significant new policy. From that date forward interest yields on bonds issued after October 1947 will earn a variable rate of interest with a guaranteed minimum depending on general market interest rates.

Under this plan, Series EE bonds, outstanding Series E bonds and savings notes earn 85 percent of the average market yield on five-year treasury securities during the bond's lifetime, compounded semiannually, as long as the bonds are held for five years or longer. If market rates rise, savings bonds will keep pace with them. If market rates decline, savings bonds are guaranteed under this new plan to earn no less than 7.5 percent when held five years or longer. If the bonds are cashed in less than five years from the date they are issued, they will earn fixed guaranteed interest rates. You can find out more about this new feature of savings bonds by contacting your local bank or savings and loan association.

Mutual Funds

Investing in mutual funds is a way of depending on the experts to pick your investment portfolio for you. A mutual fund is an investment company that pools capital invested by many individuals and, in turn, invests that pool of capital in various ways in the stock market, bonds, money market securities, etc. A mutual fund, therefore, can achieve greater diversification than an average investor can.

The fund assumes the responsibility of managing its total capital. You as an individual investor do not have to decide what to buy, when to buy, or when to sell.

One advantage of mutual funds is their low cost. Managing your own investment portfolio can be expensive, but mutual funds, because of their size, usually require low rates on brokerage commissions. The management fee for

most funds is about one half of one percent per year. And many funds allow you to invest as little as $25.

There is a great variety in the kinds of mutual funds available, from quite conservative to highly speculative. Some are purely stock funds, others are purely bond funds, others may specialize only in convertible bonds. Basically, you should choose a mutual fund based on these main areas of interest:

- Its investment objectives (growth, income, and so on).
- Its management.
- Its track record.

In the fund's history, pay special attention to those periods of time when the stock market was down. A good investment fund is one that has shown its ability to protect its capital during down markets.

An added "guardian angel" is a third-party timing service. If, for example, you are invested in a mutual fund that is always "fully invested" in stocks, you are exposing yourself to the possibility of a decline in the value of your investment if the market falls. A third-party timing service moves your capital into a money market account if it appears the market is heading down, and moves you back into the stock fund if it looks as though the market is heading back up. As with a mutual fund, you should investigate timing services, including past performance records, before making a decision. Fees for a timing service are generally around two percent per year.

NOTE: Overall, the stock market certainly is not the place for all your capital. However, if gone about in the proper way, investing in the market can prove to be very rewarding. As with all aspects of your financial picture, it's a good idea to discuss your situation with a trusted financial planner, stockbroker, or informed friend before making any decisions.

HOW LONG WILL YOUR
SAVINGS LAST?

Many people wonder how long their savings will last once they retire. The chart below shows how many years you can expect to use your investments as income. To use the chart, first determine what percentage of your *original* capital you'll want to withdraw each year. Then find the average interest rate you expect your money will earn during your retirement. This will then give you the number of years you can expect your savings to last. For example, if when you retire you decide to withdraw 10 percent of your *original* capital each year and the return on your investment averages 8 percent, you can expect your principal to last about twenty years. (Where the chart is blank, at this combination of withdrawal and investment earnings your capital will never be exhausted.)

Percentage of Original Savings/Investments Withdrawn Annually	Average Annual Growth Rate/Return on Investments										
	5%	6%	7%	8%	9%	10%	11%	12%	13%	14%	15%
2%											
4%											
6%	36										
7%	25	33									
8%	20	23	30								
9%	16	18	22	28							
10%	14	15	17	20	26						
11%	12	13	14	16	19	25					
12%	11	11	12	14	15	18	23				
13%	9	10	11	12	13	15	17	21			
14%	9	10	10	11	12	13	15	17	21		
15%	8	9	9	10	11	12	13	14	17	21	
16%	7	8	8	9	10	10	11	12	14	16	20
18%	6	6	7	7	8	8	8	8	9	9	10
20%	5	6	6	6	6	7	7	7	8	8	8

The "Investment Rule of 72"

Take the number 72 and divide it by the annual interest rate you can get on your capital investment. This number will tell you how many years it will take for your initial investment to double.

This chart shows the results that an account which has one dollar deposited in it each year for a specific number of years would earn at a set interest rate. For example: If you deposited $1 each year for 10 years at 5% interest, you would have a total of $13.21 at the end of 10 years.

You can use this chart for any amount you might wish to save. Let's assume you can save $50 per month and you have 15 years until you retire. Let's also assume you locate a savings account that pays 8% interest.

You would figure the amount you would have when you retire like this: Find the 15 year row and the 8% column. It shows that $1 invested each year for 15 years at 8% interest will earn a total of $29.32. You'll be investing $600 per year ($50 per month x 12 months). So, if $1 per year for 15 years at 8% interest earns $29.32, $600 per year for 15 years at 8% interest will earn $600 x $29.32 or $17,592.

Year	3%	4%	5%	6%	7%	8%	9%	10%	12%	15%
1	1.03	1.04	1.05	1.06	1.07	1.08	1.09	1.10	1.12	1.15
2	2.09	2.12	2.15	2.18	2.21	2.25	2.28	2.31	2.37	2.47
3	3.18	3.25	3.31	3.37	3.44	3.51	3.57	3.64	3.78	3.99
4	4.31	4.42	4.53	4.64	4.75	4.87	4.98	5.11	5.35	5.74
5	5.47	5.63	5.80	5.98	6.15	6.34	6.52	6.72	7.12	7.75
6	6.66	6.90	7.14	7.39	7.65	7.92	8.20	8.49	9.09	10.07
7	7.89	8.21	8.55	8.90	9.26	9.64	10.03	10.44	11.23	12.73
8	9.16	9.58	10.03	10.49	10.98	11.49	12.03	12.58	13.78	15.79
9	10.46	11.01	11.58	12.18	12.82	13.49	14.19	14.94	16.55	19.30
10	11.81	12.49	13.21	13.97	14.78	15.65	16.56	17.53	19.65	23.35

Continued on page 118

Year	3%	4%	5%	6%	7%	8%	9%	10%	12%	15%
11	13.19	14.03	14.92	15.87	16.89	17.98	19.14	20.38	23.13	28.00
12	14.62	15.63	16.71	17.88	19.14	20.50	21.95	23.52	27.03	33.35
13	16.09	17.29	18.60	20.02	21.55	23.21	25.02	26.97	31.39	39.50
14	17.60	19.02	20.58	22.28	24.13	26.15	28.36	30.77	36.28	46.58
15	19.16	20.82	22.66	24.67	26.89	29.32	32.00	34.95	41.75	54.72
16	20.76	22.70	24.84	27.21	29.84	32.75	35.97	39.54	47.88	64.08
17	22.41	24.65	27.13	29.91	33.00	36.45	40.30	44.60	54.75	74.84
18	24.12	26.67	29.54	32.76	36.38	40.45	45.02	50.16	62.44	87.21
19	25.87	28.78	32.07	35.79	40.00	44.76	50.16	56.28	71.05	101.44
20	27.68	30.97	34.72	38.99	43.87	49.42	55.76	63.00	80.70	117.81
21	29.54	33.25	37.51	42.39	48.01	54.46	61.87	70.40	91.50	136.63
22	31.45	35.62	40.43	46.00	52.44	59.89	68.53	78.54	103.60	158.28
23	33.43	38.08	43.50	49.82	57.18	65.76	75.79	87.50	117.16	183.17
24	35.46	40.65	46.73	53.86	62.25	72.11	83.70	97.35	132.33	211.79
25	37.55	43.31	50.11	58.16	67.68	76.95	92.32	108.18	149.33	244.71
26	39.71	46.08	53.67	62.71	73.48	86.35	101.72	120.10	168.37	282.57
27	41.93	48.97	57.40	67.53	79.70	94.34	111.97	133.21	189.70	326.10
28	44.22	51.97	61.32	72.64	86.35	102.97	123.14	147.63	213.58	376.17
29	46.58	55.08	65.44	78.06	93.46	112.28	135.31	163.49	240.33	433.75
30	49.00	58.33	69.76	83.80	101.07	122.35	148.58	180.94	270.29	499.96

IS REAL ESTATE A GOOD INVESTMENT?

In Chapter 7 we will discuss various concerns and questions you might have about selling or purchasing a home, moving to a new location, renting, or buying a condominium or cooperative. In that chapter we will discuss your home, which most people think of in more than purely financial terms.

But what about investing in real estate other than your home, purely as a financial venture? Is real estate a good investment for a person or couple preparing for their retirement? Maybe. As with any other investment, there are a number of factors to consider, some having to do with your personal financial situation and some having to do with the characteristics, location, and use of the real estate you might purchase. You should remember that although over the years real estate has steadily grown in value, it is also considered one of the least liquid forms of investment.

When a house is purchased considerable thought is usually given to location, quality of the local schools and of the neighborhood, and the condition of the building and grounds. The same judgments must be made if you are considering the purchase of a single- or multiple-family dwelling as a rental property.

A general rule of thumb is that, as a landlord, you must get at least 10 percent of the value of the property per year in rent in order to pay all your expenses and net a profit. If you are considering such an investment, be sure to include all the expenses involved in your calculations. These include taxes, maintenance costs, insurance, improvements, vacancy rates, and the inevitable demands on your time as a landlord. You should also consider the ease or

THE WIZARD OF ID — by Brant parker and Johnny hart

difficulty you might encounter in selling the property at some future time, as well as your willingness and ability to care for the property some years down the road. The maintenance tasks that you perform now with no trouble may become a burden or a significant expense when you are ten or fifteen years older.

One final factor you should consider when calculating the expense of such a venture is the return you could have earned if you had invested your equity in the best possible alternative to your real estate investment. What investment opportunities will you be passing up to make this investment and how do they compare in rate of return, safety, and liquidity?

Converting Your Home Equity to Income

For years people were told that buying a house was an investment, like putting money in the bank. But until recently there were only two recognized methods of cashing in on that investment. One was to sell the house and the other was to take out a second mortgage (borrowing against the amount of your equity—the money value of your property minus claims against it—usually at a high rate of interest for a short term).

Now, a relatively new and innovative program called "home equity conversion" has come upon the scene, and it may be the key to unlocking your biggest asset and increasing your income while allowing you to remain in your home for as long as you wish. Home equity conversions are particularly attractive to elderly homeowners. Nationally, among people sixty-five or older heading households, 72 percent own their homes. More than 80 percent of these homes are mortgage free. But as a group the elderly are becoming increasingly property-rich and income-poor.

Inflation is boosting the value of their homes but is also eroding their incomes. It's like living in a bank vault, dead broke. Many elderly homeowners have thousands of dollars of wealth on paper, yet their fixed incomes or retirement pensions aren't enough to keep them comfortably ahead of food, utility bills, taxes, home maintenance, and medical costs. What they need is cash, and cash is what they can get through a home equity conversion program.

This works like a reverse mortgage. You, the homeowner, obtain a mortgage on your property but, instead of paying the bank each month, the bank pays you.

Though there are several variations on the types of equity conversion plans, here's one basic example of how it can work. The bank approves a maximum loan amount based on the value of the house. Instead of releasing the loan in one lump sum, the bank pays it out in monthly installments to the borrower. Interest is charged only on the outstanding balance of the loan, which starts out very small.

The bank is repaid the principal of the loan, plus interest that may be due when the home is sold or when the owner dies and the estate pays off the debt.

Reverse mortgages are still in the experimental stages in most areas of the country, mainly due to the current high interest rates, but a drop in rates could open the doors to their use nationwide. It's an idea whose time is coming, if not yet wholly here.

The benefits of such a service are many, but the appeal lies mostly in an environmental and economic security that enables us to maintain our treasured state of independence and control over our own life-styles.

Here's what Jane Bryant Quinn, noted financial consultant and columnist for *Newsweek*, has to say about the home equity conversion concept.

"Retirees represent one of the country's fastest growing interest groups, and their interests are plain: They want higher incomes and greater security. Their demands might be met through bigger tax breaks, more government aid and higher Social Security benefits—all of which run the risk of laying more taxes (or more inflation) on the public at large. A better approach would be to help older people provide for themselves by putting at their service the tens of thousands of dollars they've accumulated in their houses."*

LIFE INSURANCE

The basic purpose of life insurance is to provide financial protection for your dependents in the event of your premature death. The only kind of life insurance that offers just this simple protection is known as term insurance. Under such a policy the holder is covered for the face value for a specified period of time as long as the premiums are paid. Term insurance policies have no cash value either during or at the end of the term of the policy.

Most life insurance companies offer plans that are a combination of term insurance and banking. These plans are commonly known as whole life, straight life, limited payment life, or endowment policies. They offer a method of forced savings in addition to term insurance: Part of the premium goes toward insurance and part toward a cash-value fund. As the policy matures the cash value grows, earning interest at an extremely modest rate. Policyholders can borrow against the cash value at low interest rates.

Years ago, when savings account interest rates and investment returns were very low compared to the present, no one paid too much attention to the low return on investment for an individual life insurance policy. Today, however, there is a great discrepancy between this return and the return on alternative forms of investment. Financial counselors everywhere are recommending that whole-life policyholders, if insurable, purchase term insurance, then cash in their whole-life policies and put the cash in higher-yielding money market funds, bank certificates of deposit, or other investments.

This may not be the best choice for you. The choice you make should be based on your own financial situation and should be made only after

---

*Jane Bryant Quinn, "On Reverse Mortgages." *Newsweek*, March 30, 1981.

consulting with a trusted financial advisor who does not stand to gain by steering you toward a certain course of action. You should review your life insurance situation regardless of whether or not you plan to make any changes. Do you have enough insurance? Are you overinsured now that you have fewer dependents? Do you need any insurance at all?

GOOD TAX PLANNING

Taxes are an important financial planning consideration in regard to both earned income and management of your personal investments and savings. You should always keep in mind the impact of financial decisions on your overall tax liability and the influence that taxes have on the return on your investments. For someone in the 30 percent tax bracket, for example, a tax-sheltered investment returning 8.4 percent is just as valuable as a 12 percent return on an investment that is not tax sheltered.

As you approach retirement, plan on taking maximum advantage of the fact that your taxable income will probably drop significantly from the last year of employment to the first year of retirement. You can do this by taking as many itemized deductions as possible in the last year of employment, such as prepaying charitable contributions and prepaying your state income tax. At the same time, you should shift as much taxable income as possible to the following year—your first retirement year. There will be tax advantages, for example, in opening an IRA even in the last year of employment.

Tax laws are complex and the impact of taxes on your financial decisions is significant, so this is one area where the advice of experts can be particularly helpful. A good financial planner will carefully consider your current and future tax brackets when advising you on managing your personal finances.

KNOW YOUR PENSION PLAN

More than fifty million Americans are now covered by retirement plans, including both active workers and retirees receiving a pension benefit. There is a good deal of variety among the various plans offered by employers, however, and not all of them will pay off in the glowing terms used to describe them.

The amount an individual receives from his or her pension plan upon retirement usually depends on the number of years of service and the salary

level during those working years. If you are participating in a company pension plan, your personnel department will be able to give you some idea of what your pension check will be, although an exact figure may not be available until you retire.

In 1974 a federal law known as ERISA (Employee Retirement Income Security Act) was enacted that provides a guarantee that once you have earned a pension with an employer, you cannot lose it. The law also stipulates minimum vesting standards. Vesting is your right to receive your employer's contribution on your behalf to the pension plan, with all its earned interest, when you retire, even if you stop working for that employer before you retire.

Under ERISA an employer's pension plan must, at a minimum, provide vesting under one of the following formulas:

- Vesting of 25 percent after five years, gradually increasing to full vesting after fifteen years.
- Full vesting immediately after ten years.
- Vesting of 50 percent after a worker's age and total years of service add up to forty-five, gradually increasing to 100 percent after five years or more.

The purpose of these provisions is to assure that pension benefits earned with one employer would not be lost if the worker moved to a different employer. This is particularly important today because the average man changes jobs every four and a half years and the average woman every two and a half years.

Many pension plans offer several options as to how the benefits are paid to employees. Your decision on which option, if you have any, is extremely important because once your decision is made you cannot change your mind, and your choice can significantly affect the total benefit you receive from your pension plan. Here are some typical options you might have.

1. You can take an annuity that will pay you and you alone a fixed monthly check for your lifetime.
2. You can take an annuity that will pay you a fixed monthly check for a specified period of time.
3. You can take an annuity that will pay you a fixed monthly check for your lifetime, then will continue to be paid to your spouse for his or her lifetime.
4. You can take a lump sum distribution from the retirement plan and pocket all the cash.
5. You can take a lump sum distribution and roll it over into an Individual Retirement Account (IRA).

Each of these choices has pros and cons and must be considered in light of your personal financial situation. You should consult your personnel department for details on the options available to you and talk to your own financial advisor about what's best in your situation.

When investigating pension plans you should obtain answers to the following questions:

1. What formula is used to compute your benefit?
2. How do you qualify for the plan? Is there a minimum age? Hours worked? Time with company?

3. How does Social Security affect the plan? If it's integrated with Social Security, is your income limited to a certain amount?
4. Can you make voluntary contributions to the plan?
5. If you leave the company or even move within it can you keep your current plan?
6. Are there any cost of living adjustments included in the plan?
7. Can the pension be canceled after you retire? If so, for what reason? Are there things you can do to prevent this?
8. When will you become vested in the plan?
9. Is there life insurance associated with the plan? Are there additional death benefits?
10. What are the survivor's benefits of the plan? Does it differ before and after you retire?
11. Is there any penalty for early retirement? If so, what is it?

SOCIAL SECURITY

Social Security is the nation's basic method of providing a continuing income when an individual's or family's earnings are reduced or stopped because of retirement, disability, or death. Social Security was designed to provide retirees with a "floor of protection": you should consider it as only a portion of your retirement income, and assume that more than half of your total retirement income will come from other sources. Over 95 percent of U.S. workers, now including federal employees, are contributing to Social Security and will be eligible to collect benefits when they retire or another need arises.

When Social Security was enacted in 1935, it covered workers only, and only when they retired. Through the years it has expanded to cover survivors and certain dependents of retired workers. Disability benefits have been added for workers who become severely disabled before age sixty-five. (You are considered disabled if you have a severe physical or mental condition that prevents you from working and is expected to last, or has lasted, for at least twelve months, or is expected to result in death.) Later, Social Security expanded to include Medicare, which provides basic hospital and medical insurance protection for people sixty-five and over.

WHO CAN COLLECT SOCIAL SECURITY?

The Social Security Administration must decide on an individual basis who is eligible to receive benefits. The following groups of people may be eligible for a monthly Social Security check:

- Retired workers (are entitled to benefits from the first full month they are sixty-two).
- Disabled workers.
- Unmarried children of retired, disabled, or deceased workers if they are under eighteen (or under nineteen if full-time high school students). Payments made to children up to the age of twenty-two if in college have been eliminated.

- Retired, disabled, or deceased worker's unmarried children eighteen or over who were severely disabled before age twenty-two and who continue to be disabled.
- Retired or disabled worker's wife or dependent husband, age sixty-two or over.
- Wife or husband under age sixty-two if she or he is caring for a child under sixteen (or disabled) who's getting a benefit based on the retired or disabled worker's earnings.
- Worker's widow or widower age sixty or older.
- Worker's widow or widower, or surviving divorced mother or father if caring for the worker's child under age sixteen (or disabled) who is getting a benefit based on the earnings of the deceased worker.
- Deceased worker's dependent parents age sixty-two or older.
- Widow or widower 50 or older who becomes disabled not later than seven years after mother's or father's benefits end.
- A divorced spouse at 62 or over, or a surviving divorced spouse fifty or older if the marriage lasted ten years or more.
- Beginning in January of 1985, eligible divorced spouses at sixty-two regardless of whether the former spouse has retired or is receiving benefits, provided the divorce has been in effect at least two years.

WHEN SHOULD YOU CONTACT SOCIAL SECURITY?

Social Security is not paid to you automatically. You must apply for benefits at your Social Security district office. Here are the times when it is important to contact Social Security:

- If you become unable to work because of an illness or injury that is expected to last a year or longer.
- Soon after age sixty to get benefit estimate and information.
- A few months before you reach age sixty-two if you plan to retire at sixty-two, or a few months before you retire if you are over sixty-two, to actually apply for benefits.
- A few months before reaching age sixty-five—to sign up for Medicare—even if you are still working (unless you are getting a Social Security check when you turn sixty-five, in which case Medicare enrollment is automatic).
- If someone in your family dies.

Call your local Social Security office to find out what documents you need to bring with you to apply for benefits.

Qualifying For Benefits

Before you can get retirement checks, you must have credit for a certain amount of work covered by Social Security. The exact amount depends on your age. The following table shows in years how much credit is needed for retirement benefits:

WORK CREDIT FOR
RETIREMENT BENEFITS

If you reach age 62 in	Years you Need
1983	8
1987	9
1991 or later	10

Calculation of Benefits

The formula used by the Social Security system for determining the amount of benefits is designed to replace a certain percentage of your immediate preretirement income. Lower-paid employees will receive a greater percentage of their preretirement income than average wage earners, who in turn receive a higher percentage than high wage earners. These percentage rates, called replacement rates, are scheduled to be reduced gradually over the next few years. Even though the benefit is weighted to give low-paid workers a greater percentage of their preretirement income, the formula still preserves the principle of basing benefits on contributions. The benefits are related to average wages earned. A worker who has paid the maximum Social Security taxes will receive a larger benefit than one who has paid lower taxes. So, though payments to low-paid workers represent a larger percentage of preretirement income than do payments to highly paid workers, those payments amount to fewer actual dollars.

There is no longer a fixed minimum benefit for workers who reach sixty-two, become disabled, or die after 1981. All benefit rates for workers and their dependents and survivors will be based entirely on the worker's earnings. There is one exception: Members of religious orders who have taken a vow of poverty will continue to qualify for a minimum benefit if they first become eligible for benefits before 1992.

Cost-of-Living Increases

Legislation enacted in 1972 provides for Social Security benefits to increase automatically as the cost of living rises. This cost of living adjustment occurs each year when the cost of living as measured in the previous year goes up by a certain percentage. Thus the buying power of your Social Security check is protected against inflation.

What About Early Retirement?

Early retirement? You're the only person who can really make this decision. It depends on your personal circumstances. A company pension, for instance, may influence your decision. Your ability to continue in your present line of work or to change jobs may be an important consideration. Your overall financial standing will likely be an important factor, as will your health.

If you are considering early retirement, you should be aware that although you can begin collecting Social Security as early as age sixty-two, your monthly check will be permanently reduced if you begin to collect benefits before age sixty-five. The size of the reduction depends on the number of months you receive checks before you reach sixty-five. For example, if you began collecting

at age sixty-two you would receive 80 percent of the full benefit for your earnings level; at sixty-three you would receive 86.66 percent; and at age sixty-four you would receive 93.33 percent. Regardless of when you retire, the benefit level you begin with will remain fixed for as long as you receive checks, except for the cost of living increases mentioned earlier.

Another factor to consider before making your decision is this: if you work past the age of sixty-five, your monthly benefit will be increased by 3 percent for each year (0.25 percent for each month) that you don't get a benefit.

Social Security at Sixty-two or Sixty-five?

Many people wonder about the advantages and disadvantages of taking benefits at sixty-two as opposed to sixty-five. Here is how it works out on a *strictly financial basis:**

Example:
    100% Benefit (if elected at 65): $500/mo.
     80% Benefit (if elected at 62): $400/mo.
                                    $100 Difference

Therefore, *the permanent monthly loss is $100.*
However, if benefits are claimed at 62 the worker would receive:
$400/mo. × 36 mos. = $14,400 *before* age 65. (plus cost of living)

$100)$14,400 = 144 mos., or 12 years
(per month   +
permanent loss)   age 65
                             _____
                              77 is
                        "Break Even" Age

In other words, a worker must live past age seventy-seven before he or she begins to lose money for having elected benefits at sixty-two. *This formula applies no matter what the amount of the monthly benefit because it is based on relative percentages.*

---

*SOURCE: Valerie S. Nixon, Field Representative, Social Security Administration, Binghamton, New York District Office.

Social Security "Retirement Age"

In order to assure the future stability of the Social Security system, the age of eligibility for unreduced retirement benefits—generally referred to as the "retirement age"—will be increased from sixty-five to sixty-seven in very gradual steps starting in the year 2000. The chart below shows the age at which full retirement benefits will be paid.

AGE FOR FULL RETIREMENT BENEFITS

If You Were Born In	Retirement Age (year/months)
1938	65/2
1939	65/4
1940	65/6
1941	65/8
1942	65/10
1943–1954	66/0
1955	66/2
1956	66/4
1957	66/6
1958	66/8
1959	66/10
1960 and after	67/0

Once this change is fully phased in, a worker could still receive benefits at sixty-two, as now; but the benefit rate will be lower than the rate at age sixty-two under present law. Now, a person retiring at sixty-two receives 80 percent of the amount payable at sixty-five. When the increase in the retirement age becomes fully effective, a worker retiring at age sixty-two will get a benefit equal to 70 percent of the age sixty-seven benefit.

Limits on Earnings from Work

As a retirement benefit, Social Security is designed to help compensate for wages no longer received from employment. Income you receive from personal savings, investments, pensions, and insurance will not affect your monthly checks, but if you work for wages, your Social Security could be affected. The general rule is that, if you earn more than the annual exempt amount, your Social Security check will be reduced one dollar for each two dollars you earn above the exempt amount.

Contact your local Social Security office to find out the exempt amount you can earn each year. Beginning in 1990, one dollar in benefits will be withheld for each three dollars of earnings above the exempt amount for persons age sixty-five and over.

Taxation of Social Security Benefits

Beginning in 1984, a portion of a person's Social Security benefit will be included in his or her taxable income if the person's adjusted gross income, plus nontaxable interest income and half of his or her Social Security benefits, is

more than a base amount. The base amount for an individual is $25,000; for a couple filing jointly it is $32,000; for a couple filing separately, it is zero. The amount of benefits to be included in taxable income will be the lesser of:

- One-half of the benefits for the year, or
- One-half of the excess of the person's combined income—adjusted gross income plus one-half of benefits—over the base amount.

Beginning in 1984, Social Security will send you an annual statement of benefits received to help you in filing your income taxes.

Direct Deposit—Security and Convenience

You can have your checks automatically deposited in your checking or savings account in a bank, savings bank, savings and loan association, credit union, or similar institution. Here are some advantages to direct deposit into your bank account:

- You don't have to stand in line to cash or deposit your check.
- If you are away from home, your money is available in your account instead of sitting in your mailbox.
- You don't have any problems cashing your check.
- You don't have to worry about losing your check or having it stolen.

THE IMPORTANCE OF KEEPING GOOD RECORDS

As you approach retirement—five years, ten years, fifteen years away—you may want to organize personal records if they are not in good order. This can include an inventory of your assets (large and small), location of valuable papers, your investment and savings plan, and an operating budget. The value of your present estate and its potential for growth (or loss) will make a difference in the kind of record keeping and planning you may need. But whether your estate is large or small the principle is the same—looking ahead, assessing your needs and possibilities, and making plans for the greatest possible income and freedom for personal activities. Another important point:

For married people, this is a matter that should involve both partners. If financial planning has been a solo operation, start your own educational program so that you and your spouse are both knowledgeable about this important topic.

FINDING AND USING A FINANCIAL ADVISOR

Early in this chapter, we advised strongly that you consider seeking professional advice to help you plan and make financial decisions. A professional advisor should never be considered a substitute for being well informed yourself, but he or she can certainly help guide you through the complexities of personal finances. Consult experts in financial planning to benefit from their technical knowledge and experience, but remember that it's your money, and you are the person who can best understand your own financial needs.

The ideal financial advisor will give you objective advice and guidance at a reasonable cost, which may be partly or totally tax deductible. If possible, you should choose a financial advisor who works on a fee-for-service basis rather than on commission, because this is the best way to ensure that the advice you are given will be objective.

The best way to find a competent financial advisor is by referral from a friend or business associate who has worked with that individual. Once you have found an advisor, sit down for an hour or so together and get to know the person. Don't be afraid to ask about professional credentials and for the names of several clients you can contact for references.

IS THERE VALUE IN "CRASH PLANNING"?

Is it ever too late to plan your retirement finances? Certainly there is a point as you draw nearer to retirement when there simply is not enough time left to take action that will significantly affect your retirement finances. But that point may be nearer to retirement than you think—and it will vary according to your particular financial situation. You may, perhaps, be in better financial shape than you imagine. But it is extremely important that you get out a pencil and paper and determine exactly where you stand. A number of people have made late starts in providing financial security for their retirement years and yet have managed to do a good job. Even for these fortunate people, though, the first step was to determine their situation exactly. Then they could set goals for themselves based on their expected future needs. Finally, they could devise a plan that enabled them to reach their goals.

SITUATIONS TO CONSIDER

Following are a number of situations that pose problems related to the subject of this chapter. There are no right or wrong "answers" to these situations. They are presented simply to stimulate your thinking about retirement and to

emphasize certain aspects of retirement planning. It is not necessary to arrive at any particular conclusion about each case.

It's a good idea for couples to review the situations separately and then share their thoughts. If you are single, perhaps you have a friend, relative, or clergyman with whom you can exchange ideas. Discussing situations like these can help to clarify key aspects of retirement planning and will enable you to become more in tune with your feelings and those of others.

Situation 1: Early Retirement: Will Income Be Sufficient?

Mike is tired of the rat race and thinks he might like to retire next year at the age of sixty-two. The trouble is, he's not sure he'll have enough income for him and his wife to live on comfortably. He knows his pension check and his Social Security check will be lower if he retires early but he doesn't know how much he will get. What should he do?

Possible Approaches

1. Get comparative estimates (early versus late retirement) of his Social Security and pension benefits.
2. After estimating his retirement income, try living on that amount for six months to see how it works out.
3. Take early retirement and go on a tight budget—other opportunities will open up.
4. Don't retire early. Open an IRA and save for three more years to ensure a comfortable retirement.
5. Retire at sixty-two and look for a part-time job.

Thoughts to Consider

1. Have you ever considered early retirement?
2. What are some of the pros and cons of early retirement?
3. Which do you think is more important—to get out of the rat race or to be financially secure? What alternatives would you consider?

Situation 2: What to Do with Insurance

Frank and Mary plan to retire in five years when Frank is sixty-two. Since the early days of their marriage they have been paying premiums on a straight life insurance policy with a face value of $25,000. The cash value of the policy is about $16,000 now and will be almost $20,000 when they retire. They don't want to pay premiums on the policy after they retire because their income won't be very high. What should they do?

Possible Approaches

1. Cash in the policy now, buy term insurance and invest the money in something that will earn a higher rate of interest.
2. Convert the policy to an annuity with survivor benefits and start drawing monthly payments when they retire.
3. Convert it to a paid-up policy when they retire.
4. Start receiving cash value in installments when they retire.

Thoughts to Consider

1. What exactly is an annuity? A paid-up life insurance policy?
2. Who do you rely upon for advice and to help plan your financial future?
3. Is there a point at which there is no longer a good reason to continue carrying life insurance? When might that be?
4. Would Frank and Mary receive a higher yield if the policy were cashed in and the money reinvested?

Situation 3: Putting Money to Work

When Marty was left a widower recently he found himself with $50,000 from insurance policies on his deceased wife. Not needing extra income now, Marty wants to invest the $50,000 wisely for his retirement. What should he do?

Possible Approaches

1. Put it all in an insured bank certificate of deposit.
2. Invest it all in blue chip stocks and bonds to keep up with inflation.
3. Open up a money market account with a brokerage firm or a bank.
4. Look for tax-sheltered investments.
5. Sit down and discuss his options with a certified financial planner.

Thoughts to Consider

1. Which do you think is more important—a low, safe yield or a high, risky yield? Why?
2. What are some "safe" investments where the yield is fairly high?
3. How would you locate and choose a financial planner?
4. Given the high rate of inflation, does it pay to save money?

Situation 4: Income and Expenses Don't Match

Jerry and Florence have been examining their financial situation in anticipation of Jerry's retirement in three years. Jerry's employer doesn't have a pension plan so their only sources of income will be from their Social Security benefits, an insurance policy they will convert to an annuity, and interest from their $10,000 savings account. They estimate that their total income will be about $850 per month and their expenses will be about $1,000 per month. Their home, which they own free and clear, has a market value of $42,000. How can they bridge the gap between their expected income and expenditures?

Possible Approaches

1. Sell their house, rent an apartment, and invest the equity from their home to produce more income.
2. Take out another mortgage on their home and invest the money in the stock market until they retire, then pay the mortgage off and bank any profits.
3. Cash in the insurance policy now and invest in high-yield savings or an IRA.
4. Re-examine their budget and cut down.
5. Jerry should plan on getting some work when he retires.

Thoughts to Consider

1. What are the financial advantages and disadvantages of selling a home to rent an apartment?
2. Would a cash savings program help Jerry and Florence?
3. Is it possible to cut down on expenses with inflation as high as it is?
4. How wise is it to remortgage one's house as a retiree? List some pros and cons of a late mortgage.

Pros   Cons

Situation 5: Gambling or Financial Planning

Emma worries about the future. Her husband, John, earns a good salary but he invests sporadically and plays the stock market on tips from friends, sometimes doing well and other times losing large amounts of money. It's difficult to get John to talk about finances and the future. What should Emma do?

Possible Approaches

1. Let John handle the money, he earns it.
2. Urge John to consult a professional financial planner.
3. Start a savings plan of her own from money taken from her household accounts.
4. Insist that John explain their financial status and consult her on future investments.

Thoughts to Consider

1. Is it a good idea to follow tips on the stock market from friends?
2. Other than the stock market, what investments could John and Emma make? How do you decide on investments?
3. How often do you review or add to your investment plan?
4. Do you think many couples jointly plan for their financial future? Why or why not?
5. How might a financial planner help John and Emma?

REFERENCES AND RESOURCES

Barnes, John. *More Money for Your Retirement.* New York: Harper & Row, 1978.

Egen, Jack. *Your Complete Guide to IRA's and Keogh's: The Simple, Safe Tax Deferred Way to Future Financial Security.* New York: Harper & Row, 1982.

Himber, Louis. *Dollars and Sense After 60.* New York: Federation of Protestant Welfare Agencies (281 Park Ave. South, 10010).

Jorgensen, James. *Your Retirement Income.* New York: Charles Scribner's Sons, 1982.

Kauffman, Alvin B. *Don't Retire Poor: How to Beat Inflation.* Woodland Hills, Calif.: A.B. Kauffman Publishers, 1982.

LeClair, R.T. *Money and Retirement: How to Plan for Lifetime Financial Security.* Reading, Mass.: Addison-Wesley, 1982.

Marketing Your Skills After Retirement. New York: World Trade Academy Press, 1974.

National Center for Home Equity Conversion, 110 East Main, Rm. 1010, Madison, WI 53703.

Phillips, Carole. *The Money Workbook for Women.* New York: Arbor House, 1982.

Porter, Sylvia. *Sylvia Porter's New Money Book for the 80's.* New York: Doubleday, 1979.

Quinn, Jane Bryant. *Everyone's Money Book.* New York: Delacorte Press, 1979.

Rosefsky, Robert A. *Money Talks.* New York: John Wiley & Sons, 1982.

Schandel, Terry K. *Tax Tactics for the Retired.* New York: Atheneum, 1982.

Tucker, James F. *Buying Treasury Securities at Federal Banks.* Federal Reserve Bank of Richmond, 1980.

Van Caspel, Venita. *Money Dynamics for the 1980's.* Reston, Va.: Reston Publishing Co., 1980.

————. *The Power of Money Dynamics.* Reston, Va.: Reston Publishing Co., 1983.

Warach, Bernard. *The Older American Survival Guide.* New York: Prentice-Hall, 1981.

Chapter 6
Planned Spending

CHAPTER 6 WARM-UP

Before reading "Planned Spending," test your knowledge of the subject by placing a check mark next to the answer you prefer. Check the key at the end to find the correct answer.

1. It doesn't matter whether you have a spending plan or not. You'll spend the same anyway.   True_____ False_____

2. Everyone should have a personal allowance.   True_____ False_____

3. The average cost of owning, operating, and insuring an automobile is about thirty cents for each mile driven, and rising.   True_____ False_____

4. Products or services that appear to be "too good to be true" are usually gyps.   True_____ False_____

5. If your credit purchases total more than 15 to 20 percent of your income (excluding a mortgage) you're heading for a financially dangerous situation.   True_____ False_____

6. You should always maintain an emergency fund equal to at least one month's earnings.   True_____ False_____

7. The annual percentage rate is the amount of principal you repay monthly in a credit agreement.   True_____ False_____

8. Many merchants offer discounts to persons sixty-five and over.   True_____ False_____

9. Expenses for one person living alone are roughly half of expenses for a couple.   True_____ False_____

10. The Equal Credit Opportunity Act bars discrimination on the basis of age.   True_____ False_____

Key: 1. (F), 2. (T), 3. (T), 4. (T), 5. (T), 6. (T), 7. (F), 8. (T), 9. (F), 10. (T).

THE WIZARD OF ID   by Brant parker and Johnny hart

THE WIZARD OF ID by Brant parker and Johnny hart

PLANNED SPENDING

For many people the word *budget* sounds negative. It may imply severe limitations and inferior-quality merchandise, or it may suggest the idea of not being able to afford what you want. That's an unfortunate association. Because a budget can offer just the opposite—it can maximize your ability to spend money in such a way that you have the things you want and need most.

A budget is simply a spending plan. It gives you the opportunity to see where your money is going, and allows you to allocate your money so that you have enough for the things you want, be they practical or fanciful.

Maybe you use a spending plan now, or have in the past. Or maybe you never worked one out. Whatever the case, it is important in view of retirement to prepare a new spending plan, for new financial circumstances will likely change some of your spending habits. Consider these circumstances:

- Your retirement income will probably be less than your present income.
- Your retirement income will be fairly fixed. True, if you plan to draw Social Security benefits, these benefits will include a cost of living adjustment. But the rest of your income, including your pension, cannot be counted on to keep up with rising costs of living.
- The present rate of inflation, as it continues, will severely diminish the buying power of your income and savings over the coming years.

Since you will probably have less income in retirement and since the value of your money will be diminishing, careful planning now is important so that the money you do have can be spent wisely.

Usually, the older we get, the better we understand what we really want and need, and the more we know about how to do things economically. Retirees have more time to plan what they want and can take time to "shop around" for the best prices. For these reasons you have the potential to be a far better consumer in retirement than you were while employed. You may be surprised at how much you actually can afford, even on a relatively fixed income, if you take the time to plan your spending.

This chapter will show you how, through keeping a spending plan and buying wisely, you can make your retirement dollar work harder for you. Specifically we will examine the steps in drawing up a spending plan and projecting income and expenses, and we will explore simple and practical ways to reduce your consumer costs.

WHERE DOES YOUR MONEY GO?

As a group, today's retirees have more money to spend than ever before. Many Americans are taking early retirement, and farsighted ones give early and careful thought to their financial retirement plan. Then why, from the top to the bottom of the economic ladder, do so many retirees ask, "Where does the money go?" One answer is that our skills in managing money have not kept pace with the complexity of today's economy.

Your spending plan should be a flexible guide. You won't find one already mapped out in a money management book somewhere, because to be effective it must reflect *you*—your needs, your wants, your plans. Your spending plan cannot be carved in stone; but it *can* be used as a master plan that (with willpower and determination) will put you on a sound financial footing.

Start with where you are today. Take a look at your present income and expenses and your current net worth. Your strongest earning years are usually between the ages of forty and sixty-five. These are the years when many of us see a decline in family obligations, which frees up extra money to be invested in securing our future.

After you have a good idea of what income you have, the next step is to find out where it's going: no guesswork, just all the hard facts. Get out your canceled checks and financial records for the past year and take a careful accounting. *If you don't know where your money goes, you have very little chance of getting it to go where you want it to.* And this is why a lot of people become discouraged and stray from their plans and goals.

Now is the time to give careful thought to your total financial picture, from where you are now to where you want to be in retirement. Remember, you're in control. And don't be afraid to experiment with plans until you find the one that works best for you.

YOUR RETIREMENT SPENDING PLAN

For purposes of comparison, you may be interested in this spending estimate for an "average" retired couple, based on percentages of total retirement income.

Housing	27–35%
Food	19–25%
Transportation	14–17%
Clothing	9–13%
Medical	6– 7%
Recreation	4– 5%
Personal	2– 4%
Tobacco and Alcohol	1– 2%

Your total expenses in retirement should be no more than 75 percent of your current expenses. You can evaluate your proposed retirement spending plan by reviewing the following items.

- A spending plan should express your wants as well as your needs. For some, travel expenses may comprise a considerable part of a budget; for others, eating out more often may be preferred. If you're not allowing yourself money to do some things that you've always dreamed about doing, your spending plan should be looked at again to see where expenses can be shifted.
- A spending plan should be simple. Unless you have the habit of falling into debt easily, it isn't necessary to examine your expenditures daily, weekly, or biweekly. Monthly accounting is more reasonable. But be sure to keep receipts and canceled checks for your expenses.
- A spending plan should be flexible. You may discover in retirement that certain expenses are not as high as you anticipated, while others are higher. The costs of clothing, transportation, and leisure-time activities may be particularly hard to project. You will, therefore, want to evaluate and revise your plan when you see how your circumstances and needs have changed. The important thing, however, you will already have learned—the principles and importance of living within a spending plan.

PLANNING TOOL

Planned Spending Now and in Retirement

You may find this difficult to fill out at first, because you've probably made purchases and paid bills without keeping a record. Take some time to gather what records you have, try to reflect back and project forward a few years for major expenses that may need to be planned for. Then, begin to formulate your plan for more successful money management.

INCOME

	Now	In Retirement
Salary:		
You	_____	_____
Spouse	_____	_____
Social Security Benefits:		
You	_____	_____
Spouse	_____	_____

INCOME (*Continued*)

	Now	In Retirement
Pension Benefits:		
You	_____	_____
Spouse	_____	_____
Investments:		
Interest on Savings	_____	_____
Interest on Bonds	_____	_____
Stock Dividends	_____	_____
Real Estate Income	_____	_____
Insurance Annuity	_____	_____
Company Profit Sharing	_____	_____
Other (List)	_____	_____
	_____	_____
	_____	_____
Total Monthly Income:	_____	_____

EXPENSES

	Now	In Retirement
Housing:		
Mortgage or Rent	_____	_____
Utilities	_____	_____
Fuel	_____	_____
Maintenance & Repairs	_____	_____
Insurance	_____	_____
Taxes	_____	_____
Food:		
At Home	_____	_____
Away From Home	_____	_____
Clothing:	_____	_____
Medical/Dental:	_____	_____
Transportation:		
Auto Loan	_____	_____
Gas & Oil	_____	_____
Insurance	_____	_____
Repairs	_____	_____
Telephone:	_____	_____
Furniture:	_____	_____
Appliances:	_____	_____
Insurance:		
Life	_____	_____
Health	_____	_____

EXPENSES (*Continued*)

	Now	In Retirement
Income Taxes:	_____	_____
Working Expenses:	_____	_____
Outstanding Loans:	1. _____	1. _____
	2. _____	2. _____
	3. _____	3. _____
Credit Card Charges:	1. _____	1. _____
	2. _____	2. _____
	3. _____	3. _____
Recreation:	_____	_____
Personal Items:	_____	_____
Savings:	1. _____	1. _____
	2. _____	2. _____
	3. _____	3. _____
Other:	_____	_____
Total Monthly Expenses:	_____	_____

EMERGENCY FUNDS

To help ensure the success of your financial plans and to help meet the unexpected future expenses that crop up for all of us, you may want to establish an emergency fund. You don't have to keep a lot of money in such a fund, but it should be enough to cover a minimum of one month's living expenses.

This emergency fund is not a savings fund. It is not to be used to plan expenditures, or as a source of extra income. It is simply a fund to tide you over during temporary emergencies that could wreak havoc with your normal flow of income and expenses.

When you have determined the amount of money to put aside in your emergency fund, start a monthly payment plan to establish it. Once the fund is established, you should literally forget about it until a truly unplanned-for and necessary expense arises.

MONEY MANAGEMENT TOOLS

We take tools for granted in all aspects of life, from basic food preparation to education to building and so on. But do you know the basic tools you need to manage your money skillfully? If used regularly, the following planning tools will save you time, energy, and money.

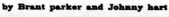

1. **An inventory of valuable papers**—This inventory will include a listing of the real and personal property you own, financial account numbers, deeds, bills of sale, insurance policies, contracts, stock or bond certificates, birth certificates, marriage licenses, wills, etc. The inventory also lists *where* each of these valuable papers is located.

2. **A "net-worth" statement**—This is a listing of what you own and what you owe on a particular day. The difference between the total value of things owned and those owed is your net worth. This is an excellent tool for revealing your total financial picture on a yearly basis. By comparing statements you can see growth or decline in your financial standing and set goals for the coming year.

3. **An action plan for matching your income to your expenses**—This is a list showing the payments you are obligated to make during any given month (including savings), and a matching list of the number of income sources received during the month and their amounts. Mapping out your month's income and expenses will enable you to project the most efficient use of your money.

4. **A place for keeping your financial papers**—Try to keep the papers and tools you use regularly in a comfortable, well-organized spot. Having a regular place to pay bills, review records, or locate documents makes it easier to complete your financial matters. It may be a desk, a table, or a countertop where the light is good, where you can spread your papers out and write easily. You will need a comfortable chair, pencils and paper, clips, staples, a calculator, etc. You can consider this space your financial business center.

Quiz Yourself: Buying Wisely

When you're wondering whether you should or should not buy, give yourself this quiz, prepared by the Council for Family Financial Education, and find out.

1. Do I really need this item?   YES   NO
2. Is the price reasonable?   YES   NO
3. Is this the best time to buy the item?   YES   NO
4. If this is a bargain, is it a current model (if this matters to you)?   YES   NO
5. If "on sale," is the price a true sale price?   YES   NO
6. Are you sure no less expensive item of equal quality can be substituted?   YES   NO

7. Are there any major disadvantages to purchasing
    this item?   YES   NO
8. If excessive in price, will it truly satisfy an inner
    need? (If not excessive, just check yes.)   YES   NO
9. Have you checked and researched the item
    ("comparison-shopped")?   YES   NO
10. Do you know the retailer's reputation?   YES   NO
11. Does this retailer offer any special services with the
    item (servicing, etc.)?   YES   NO

Score your answers as follows:
9–11 yes's: Buy the product.
6–8 yes's: Think again.
Fewer than 6 yes's: Forget it.

SPENDING WISELY

Taking the time to make decisions about spending priorities will help you get more for your money. Knowing what to look for in a product or service will also help you stretch your buying power. In fact, there are many ways to go about spending your money in the wisest possible fashion. Here are a few good tips:

1. Decide how much you will spend each month for various items and stick to this amount. Try living on a projected retirement spending plan for a few months *before* you retire.
2. Try to plan ahead so that large expenditures for such things as mortgages, roofing, siding or house painting, major appliances, and automobiles are out of the way before you retire.
3. Investigate methods for cutting down on utility costs. Start now to "turn off the juice when not in use" and check your home weatherization to maximize your heating dollars.
4. Study supermarket ads. When an exceptional sale on nonperishable items comes along, buy in quantity. Though your household may be small, you'll eventually use the item up.
5. An occasional impulse purchase is fun and can provide variety—but when you're on a limited income, too many will destroy your spending plan.
6. In preparing a list of projected expenses, most people underestimate the yearly cost of "little things" like gifts, cigarettes, newspapers, magazines, and the like. For this reason, try keeping track of how much you are spending for these items for a month or two before you draw up your spending plan. This record will probably surprise you and will help you to plan your budget more realistically.
7. If you have any land at all, start a "victory garden." Grow some of your own food. You'll be surprised what you can do with the smallest of spaces: many varieties of plants have been developed specifically for small gardens. Besides, gardening can be fun. It provides both exercise and satisfaction.
8. Try cooking "from scratch" more often. When you buy convenience foods, you pay dearly for the time they save you.

9. When planning to travel, you can save by investigating package deals and tours, unlimited mileage offers in trains and buses, off-season and off-hour discounts, and the like. Creativity and planning while "on the road" also can save you a great deal of money.
10. Consult consumer buying guides at your local library to check the quality of a product before making major purchases.
11. Eliminate paying interest by paying with cash or a check.
12. Rent, don't buy, items you rarely use.
13. Plan purchases to coincide with seasonal sales.
14. Check out factory outlets, discount stores, garage sales, and auctions for some super buys.
15. Pay attention to quality. You often do "get what you pay for."

A TIME-PLANNING PURCHASING TOOL

Things I Desire or Can Project I Will Need (list in priority order)	Total Cost	Amount I Need to Save Monthly (weekly)	How Long Until Purchase
1.			
2.			
3.			
4.			
5.			
6.			
7.			
8.			
9.			
10.			

CREDIT

Almost everyone is familiar with the concept of buying on credit. It's an important and necessary part of life for most of us because it allows us to make major purchases that we would otherwise be unable to make. For example, few people pay cash for their homes, car, or major appliances.

What we need always to remember about credit is that it is only rented cash. The rental fee is called interest, and it varies from one lending source to another. Interest may also depend on the degree of risk the lender believes he is taking.

According to the law, lenders must tell you the interest rate of a loan in terms of its annual percentage rate (simple interest rate). This makes it relatively easy for you to judge which lender offers you the best deal.

The Equal Credit Opportunity Act bars discrimination on the basis of age. A creditor can consider age only if:

1. You are sixty-two or over and special credit help is provided because of age.

2. The creditor uses a system favoring applicants sixty-two and over.
3. The applicant is considered to be "frail elderly" (in poor health), with questionable repayment ability.

Creditors *cannot:*

1. Refuse to consider your retirement income or money from a pension or investment plan.
2. Require you to reapply for credit after reaching a certain age or retirement.
3. Deny you credit because life insurance is not available to you.

If you believe you're being discriminated against: 1) complain in writing to the creditor, 2) get reason for denial in writing, 3) file a written complaint with the Federal Trade Commission, Equal Opportunity Division, Washington, D.C. 20580.

EVALUATE YOUR PRESENT CREDIT STATUS

Use this worksheet to analyze your present debt obligations (*not counting your mortgage*). Fill in all blanks that apply to your present situation. Get the information from your contract or credit statements.

Purpose of Loan	Amount Still Owed	Total Amount for Credit or Finance Charge	APR*	Months Left to Pay	Monthly Payment
Car	1.				
	2.				
Checking account over-draft plan	1.				
Credit cards or store charge accounts	1.				
	2.				
	3.				
	4.				
Educational debt	1.				
	2.				
Home improvement	1.				
Installment loans (bank, stores, credit union, finance co.)	1.				
	2.				
	3.				
	4.				

*Annual percentage rate

Purpose of Loan	Amount Still Owed	Total Amount for Credit or Finance Charge	APR*	Months Left to Pay	Monthly Payment
Passbook loan	1.				
Store charge accounts	1. 2. 3. 4.				
Other debts (list)	1. 2. 3. 4.				

*Annual percentage rate

Total monthly payments $_____

Monthly take-home income, $_____, divided by 7 equals $_____

If your total monthly payments is larger than one seventh (approximately 15%) of your monthly take-home pay, you may be overextending yourself with credit. You need to: (1) stop making new debts and (2) eliminate some of the debts outstanding as quickly as possible. To keep within a safe level of credit outstanding, it is recommended that individuals or families commit no more than 10% (excluding home mortgage) of monthly take-home income to credit payments.

HOW TO COMPLAIN

Have you ever bought a product and taken it home, only to find that it was defective or that you were otherwise dissatisfied with its performance or quality? If you have, then you should have complained. Consumers have a right and a duty to complain when they're dissatisfied. But how do we, or *should* we, go about it? The first step is a polite but firm phone call or visit to the business that sold you the goods or service. Explain when you bought it, what's wrong with it, and what you expect to be done about it. This first simple step should resolve your problem, but if it doesn't, the next step is to write a cool, calm, and reasonable letter of complaint.

The effectively written complaint letter can be broken down into three parts. The first paragraph should include a brief account of what happened—what you bought, where you bought it, and what is wrong with it. The second paragraph should contain a statement of what you would like to have happen. Specify whether you want the product replaced or you want your money back, for example. The third paragraph should explain what your next action will be—you'll write the attorney general's office, alert various consumer groups, contact your local paper's consumer columnist, etc.—if you don't receive satisfaction or your money back. Putting all of this in a letter may seem like a lot of trouble, but you'll find it's worth the effort.

Remember to:

1. Include your full name and address
2. Include the full name and address of the person or office you are writing to
3. Keep the letter as brief as possible
4. Keep the letter nonthreatening
5. Act positively, not angrily
6. Act while the problem is still fresh
7. Think the problem through to make sure it was not your own fault
8. Include copies of important information such as warranties, canceled checks, receipts, etc.
9. Include all facts about the problem: when and where purchased, cost, style, serial number, how you have tried dealing with the problem
10. State what you want done—money back, new part, product removed from your home, etc.
11. Always make a copy of your letter.

CAUTION: CONSUMER FRAUDS

You can protect yourself and your finances in the following ways:

- Beware of the person who calls or writes offering something for nothing—a prize, just a few minutes of your time, nothing to buy . . .
- If an "inspector" calls, do not be convinced by a badge or identification card. Shut the door while you telephone the city office or utility he or she is supposed to represent. If the person is genuine, he or she will not object to your precautions.
- Don't accept the verbal promise of salespeople in or out of stores. (This precaution applies to such items as insurance, too.) See that any payment plan or installment contract offered for your signature carries the same promises.
- Don't be hustled into signing documents. Read the fine print. If you do not understand it, don't sign. Some checking up may be in order.

- Never sign a document with blank spaces left on it. See that any details that have to be typed or written into a printed form are completed to your satisfaction before you sign.
- Telephone or call a Better Business Bureau when you suspect bad practice.
- If door-to-door solicitation is a trouble, advise your local authorities.
- Beware of "bait and switch" tactics. An advertisement for some fantastic bargain may be the bait. At the store, the salesman tries to sell you something else. "It's not much of a buy. Let me show you something better."
- Don't permit a household appliance to be taken from your home for repairs without first getting a written estimate of repair costs.
- Don't pay for a neighbor's package unless your neighbor asks you to do so. You may be paying for a box of worthless articles, an empty box, or something your neighbor never ordered.
- Don't pay a door-to-door salesman before checking his credentials.
- Don't pay a door-to-door salesman in cash. Pay him by check or money order made out to the company.
- Don't allow a door-to-door salesman to leave merchandise with you on approval. He may never come back. You may find yourself being billed for something you didn't want or need, and paying far more for it than it is worth.

The Law: Three Days to Cancel Door-to-Door Sales

On door-to-door sales of $25 or more, a Federal Trade Commission rule gives you the right to cancel your sale within three (3) days. The salesperson must:

Tell you of this right to cancel your sale.
Give you a contract or receipt.
Give you two copies of your NOTICE OF CANCELLATION.

The contract or receipt must:

1. Be in the language he or she used when talking to you;
2. be dated and show the name and address of seller;

3. contain the following statement near your (the buyer's) signature: *"You, the buyer, may cancel this transaction at any time prior to midnight of the third business day after the date of this transaction. See the attached notice of cancellation form for an explanation of this right."*

The notice of cancellation must:

1. Be in the same language he or she used when talking to you;
2. be easy to detach from the contract;
3. be completed by the seller:
   —date of sale
   —name and address of seller
   —date by which NOTICE must be sent to seller.

If you want to cancel the sale:

1. Read the notice of cancellation;
2. *Detach, sign and date* one copy and send or deliver it to the seller within three business days;
3. Keep one copy and your contract or receipt for your records.

If you cancel, the seller must, within ten days:

1. Refund all your money;
2. return any goods or property traded in;
3. cancel and return any documents that you've signed;
4. tell you whether merchandise left with you will be picked up or can be kept by you.

Within twenty days, if the seller has left goods with you:

You must:
1. Have each item available to be reclaimed in same condition as you received it,
or
2. if you agree, ship the item.

The seller must:
1. Pick up the item
or
2. pay return shipping expenses.

If the seller fails to meet any of the above requirements, he or she has violated the Federal Trade Commission rule. If you fail to do what is required of you, and the seller does what is required, YOU are responsible for all agreements in the contract.

Some door-to-door sales are *not* covered by this rule:

- Total sales costs under $25.
- Orders placed at the seller's address.
- Telephone orders.
- Sales made entirely by mail.

- Some "emergency repairs" sales.
- Real estate, insurance, or securities sales.
- Some other home repairs sales.

SEASONAL SALES CALENDAR

JANUARY

White Sales (linens, towels, blankets), Housewares & Small Appliances, Refrigerators, Freezers, Clothes Dryers, Water Heaters, Furniture (third week), Sportswear, Dresses, Furs, Handbags, Lingerie, Men's Coats, Shirts & Hats, Shoes, Cosmetics.

FEBRUARY

Furniture, Floor Covering, Bedding, Drapes & Curtains, China, Glassware, Clothes Dryers, Air Conditioners, Used Cars, Storm Windows.

MARCH

Washing Machines, Clothes Dryers, Housewares, China, Silver, Garden Supplies.

APRIL

Ranges, Washing Machines, Clothes Dryers, Cleaning Supplies, Paints, Outdoor Furniture, Dresses, Men's & Boy's Suits, Millinery, Women's & Children's Coats.

MAY

White Sales (linens, towels, blankets), Outdoor Furniture, Washing Machines, Television Sets, Air Conditioners, Fans, Lingerie, Housecoats, Summer Sportswear, Tires.

JUNE

Building Materials, Lumber, Washing Machines, Television Sets, Dresses, Piece Goods, Fabric.

JULY

Refrigerators, Freezers, Sporting Goods & Clothing, Furniture (fourth week), Children's Wear, Hosiery, Handbags, Lingerie, Men's Shirts & Hats, Shoes, Cosmetics, Millinery, Air Conditioners.

AUGUST

New Cars, Furniture, Floor Covering, Bedding, White Sales (linens, towels, blankets), Hardware, Paints, Drapes & Curtains, Air Conditioners, Furs, Men's & Boy's Suits, Men's Coats, Women's & Children's Coats, Camping Equipment.

SEPTEMBER

New Cars, Housewares, Hardware, Paints, China, Glassware, Notions, Fabrics, Batteries, Mufflers.

OCTOBER

Women's & Children's Coats, Men's & Boy's Outerwear.

NOVEMBER

Blankets, Ranges, Water Heaters, Notions, Fabrics, Women's & Children's Coats, Pre-Christmas Sales, Used Cars.

DECEMBER

Children's Wear, Men's & Boy's Suits, Women's & Children's Coats.

OTHER WAYS TO SAVE

Transportation

Normal transportation needs make up about 15 percent of an average budget. This percentage could actually increase somewhat in retirement. Of course, the daily trips to the job are no longer an expense. But now there may be more time and opportunity for travel.

The most important transportation cost is your automobile. When you estimate the cost of operating your car, be sure to consider not only the high cost of gas, but also such items as insurance, maintenance, and one factor that most of us overlook—depreciation. Some people, in their budget planning, save an amount each year that represents a car's loss in value. Then, at the end of a certain period of time, funds are available to trade the old car for a later model.

This brings up another point—does your car have to be a new car? Consider one that has been broken in for you. The first owner has taken it through its "debugging" stage, and a whopping first year's depreciation has been paid by someone else. Even older cars in excellent condition with very low mileage might be found. Also, if you don't need a lot of room so much any more, look for a smaller car that will get better gas mileage than the one you're used to.

B.C.   **by johnny hart**

Owning a car is a matter of personal need and choice. Where public transportation is good, owning a car may not be necessary. Many people have disposed of their automobiles and are using public transportation for their local daily needs. When they want to travel, they rent or lease a car. You can expect to drive a nearly new car every time you lease one. You may also find that you can use a taxi service with the money you've saved.

PLANNING TOOL

Calculating Your Annual Automobile Expenses

STEP 1. Keep records of all expenses, including purchase price, fuel, maintenance costs (oil, lubrication), repairs, replacements (tires, etc.), insurance.

STEP 2. Figure the per mile cost in the following way:
  A. Fuel—cost per gallon divided by miles per gallon obtained . . . . $_____
  B. Insurance—cost per year divided by number of miles driven per year . . . . $_____
  C. Repairs—cost per year (estimated) divided by number of miles driven per year . . . . $_____
  D. Maintenance—cost per year divided by number of miles driven per year . . . . $_____
  E. Tires—cost per set of tires divided by number of miles driven before replacement is necessary . . . . $_____
  F. Depreciation—cost of vehicle (including taxes and auto loan finance charges) divided by estimated number of miles until vehicle will be replaced . . . . $_____

STEP 3. Add the columns in Step 2. This is your cost per mile . . . $_____

STEP 4. Take the total in Step 3 and multiply it by the number of miles that you expect to drive each year. This is your yearly auto expense . . . . $_____

Income Taxes

Saving money on income taxes is done the same way in retirement as during the working years—through knowing what deductions you are eligible for and filing carefully completed returns. If you don't feel qualified or confident about doing them yourself, have a tax planner do them for you. You may want to ask for a complete explanation of the work the tax planner does so that you'll be able to do it for yourself next year. Offices of the Internal Revenue Service, some Area Agencies on Aging, and other groups offer free assistance.

Other Taxes

Many communities and school districts offer property-tax reductions to older adults. Your local county, city, or town clerk will be able to advise you about eligibility and will explain how to apply for such reductions.

Discounts

Many local merchants offer discounts to people over a certain age (usually sixty-two or sixty-five). This is often done as part of an organized, community-wide program that may also include discounts on public transportation and recreational facilities. Your Area Agency on Aging or Chamber of Commerce will have information about what is available in your community.

SITUATIONS TO CONSIDER

Following are a number of situations that pose problems related to the subject of this chapter. There are no right or wrong "answers" to these situations. They are presented simply to stimulate your thinking about retirement and to emphasize certain aspects of retirement planning. It is not necessary to arrive at any particular conclusion about each case.

It's a good idea for couples to review the situations separately and then share their thoughts. If you are single, perhaps you have a friend, relative, or clergyman with whom you can exchange ideas. Discussing situations like these can help to clarify key aspects of retirement planning and will enable you to become more in tune with your feelings and those of others.

Situation 1: Rising Utility Bills

John and Rose are troubled by rising utility bills. They can afford them right now but are wondering how they will manage three years from now when they retire. What might you suggest that John and Rose do now to prepare themselves for handling the "energy problems of the future"?

Thoughts to Consider

1. Is your home weatherized? If not, what steps can you take to reduce your energy costs?
2. Have you considered closing off parts of your home? What parts would you close?
3. Are there federal or state energy assistance programs in your area?
4. Is it possible to redecorate your home for energy efficiency (carpeting, drapes, etc.)?
5. Could alternate forms of energy be utilized (wind, solar, etc.)?
6. Does your utility company conduct home energy audits? Have you had one done?
7. Have you considered budget payment plans?
8. Where might you go to find out more about saving energy?

Situation 2: Who's Responsible?

Edna, who is four years away from retirement, has already saved over $10,000 for trips and other special things that she plans to do in retirement. Two years ago her mother had a stroke, and after a stay in the hospital, she came to live with Edna. Her mother's condition worsened, and Edna was forced to place her in a nursing home because of paralysis. After nine months in the nursing home, her mother's money is almost all spent. Now Edna is wondering about her obligations to pay for her mother's ongoing care. What is your view?

THE WIZARD OF ID   by Brant parker and Johnny hart

Possible Approaches

1. Edna is not legally responsible to pay her mother's bill and should not worry about it.
2. Edna is morally responsible and should withdraw her savings and budget her income to pay for the care.
3. Edna is legally responsible and will be sued if she doesn't pay.

Thoughts to Consider

1. Do you believe that children ought to be responsible for their parents' unpaid bills?
2. What kinds of responsibilities do children have toward their parents?
3. How could Edna's mother's care be paid for if Edna did not pay?
4. What is your state's position on children's liability for their parents' nursing home care?
5. Who, in your community, could Edna turn to for information?

Situation 3: Controlling Spending Habits

Mara is becoming concerned about her financial situation in retirement. She receives a Social Security retirement benefit and a modest pension, but needs to draw upon her savings capital each month to pay her bills. Mara has always been an impulsive shopper and she uses credit cards frequently. She has decided she must take steps to control her spending. What will help her the most?

Possible Approaches

1. Tear up the credit cards and pay cash.
2. Pay for everything by check and review her expenditures weekly.
3. Get a part-time job so she won't have to curtail her spending habits.

Thoughts to Consider

1. What are the pros and cons of buying with credit cards?
2. In inflationary times, is it better to buy with credit?
3. Do most stores and businesses accept personal checks?
4. Why do you think Mara has such a hard time controlling her purchasing habits?
5. Who might help Mara to adjust to a new way of spending?
6. How often do you use credit?

Situation 4: How Young Is Too Young?

Walt laughed when a fellow worker urged him to begin to formulate a retirement plan, saying, "I'm only forty-eight—I've got lots of time before I need to do that!" Thinking about it later, he became painfully aware that even though he has adequate insurance, he and his wife, Kathleen, have no real savings or investment plans. They have pretty much everything they want (two cars, boat, cottage, the latest home appliances), and they can travel and eat out, etc. They now feel that they should obtain one big loan to pay off their numerous debts and try to start a savings plan of some sort. How can they turn their debits into credits?

Possible Approaches

1. Sell one car, the boat, and the cottage, pay bills and start an investment plan.
2. Get a loan, pay major bills, and set up a "get-out-of-debt" plan.
3. Without borrowing, design a pay-back plan to get out of debt and start a small savings plan at the same time.
4. Do nothing. It's still too early to be worried about retirement.

Thoughts to Consider

1. Is Walt's and Kathleen's situation common today? What contributes to it?
2. How wise is it to take out a debt consolidation loan?
3. At what point should Walt and Kathleen seriously begin retirement planning?
4. Could a financial advisor help Walt and Kathleen?

Situation 5: Should You Reap What You Sow?

Pete and Marge lived according to a modest spending plan all of their working years. Now that they are retired, they have a good income and a sizable investment portfolio. Pete feels it's time to let loose a little, stop saving and begin a more liberal spending plan. Marge disagrees and feels that spending money for travel, dining out, and recreation is wasteful. Besides, Marge wants to leave their two grown children a "nice inheritance" rather than deplete what she and Pete have earned. What should Pete and Marge do?

Possible Approaches

1. Live it up! They earned the money; now it's time to enjoy it.
2. Remain on their same spending plan; the children have a right to a helping hand from their parents.
3. Stop saving and use that money for some "fanciful spending," leaving the investment portfolio intact.

Thoughts to Consider

1. Is it hard to change old spending patterns?
2. Do parents "owe" their children a financial legacy?
3. Should the children be consulted as to their wishes?
4. How do you feel about spending money on pleasurable activities and luxury items?

REFERENCES AND RESOURCES

Burkett, Larry. *The Financial Planning Workbook.* Chicago: Moody Press, 1982.

Changing Times. Editors Park, Maryland: The Kiplinger Magazine.

Cobb, C.G. *The Bad Times Primer: A Complete Guide to Survival on a Budget.* Los Angeles: Times Press, 1981.

Consumer Reports Buying Guide. Mt. Vernon, N.Y.: Consumer Union (256 Washington St., 10550).

Dissinger, Katherine. *Old, Poor, Alone and Happy: How to Live Nicely on Practically Nothing.* Chicago: Nelson-Hall, Inc., 1980.

George, Richard. *The New Consumer Survival Kit.* Boston: Little, Brown & Co., 1978.

Guide to Financial Security. Washington, D.C.: AIM (Action for Independent Maturity) (1909 K St., N.W., 20006).

Huber, Roger. *Where My Money Is Going: Income and Expense Budget.* West Newton, Pa.: Lankey Publishing Co., 1980.

Lysons, Kenneth. *Managing Your Money in Retirement.* N. Pomfret, Vt.: David & Charles, Inc., 1980.

McCullough, Bonnie. *Bonnie's Household Budget Book.* New York: St. Martin's Press, Inc., 1981.

Retirement Income and Credit, Tax Benefits for Older Americans. Washington, D.C.: Internal Revenue Service. (Check your local IRS office for other publications.)

Tax Facts. Washington, D.C.: American Association of Retired Persons (1909 K St., N.W., 20006).

Your Money's Worth in Foods. Washington, D.C.: U.S. Department of Agriculture. Available from the Superintendent of Documents, Government Printing Office, Washington, D.C. 20402.

Your Retirement Consumer Guide. Washington, D.C.: American Association of Retired Persons (1909 K St., N.W., 20006).

Chapter 7
Housing

CHAPTER 7 WARM-UP

Before reading "Where to Live," test your knowledge of the subject by placing a check mark next to the answer you prefer. Check the key at the end to find the correct answer.

1. Most retirees move to a new area when they retire.

   True_____ False_____

2. Most home-related accidents could be prevented through careful attention to home safety.

   True_____ False_____

3. Elderly homeowners in many communities are eligible for reduced property tax rates.

   True_____ False_____

4. If you sell your house after age fifty-five and don't reinvest the money in another home, you are allowed a one-time exemption on the capital gain (up to a certain amount) on your income tax return.

   True_____ False_____

5. In a cooperative housing project, you purchase a share of the corporation that owns the cooperative.

   True_____ False_____

6. In a condominium, you rent the apartment.

   True_____ False_____

7. A mobile home is an excellent investment. True_____ False_____

8. About one third of the average retired couple's income is spent on housing.

   True_____ False_____

9. Nursing homes are places where people go to die.

   True_____ False_____

10. Moving to the Sunbelt will help cure your arthritis.

    True_____ False_____

Key: 1. (F), 2. (T), 3. (T), 4. (T), 5. (T), 6. (F), 7. (F), 8. (T), 9. (F), 10. (F).

THE WIZARD OF ID   by Brant parker and Johnny hart

WHERE TO LIVE

What are your thoughts about where to live in retirement? Are you dreaming about moving to a more enjoyable climate, or about leaving a big city for the peace of country life? Or does nothing seem more attractive to you than staying where you are, close to old friends and family? Whatever your thoughts, you must take account of many factors.

There are money considerations. Housing costs have been skyrocketing recently. Government figures show that over one third of a retired couple's income is spent on housing. The kind of housing, then, that will make the most financial sense for you as a retiree is an important matter.

There are emotional considerations. Homes are not just places to reside. They are storehouses of memory. A guest room now was once a room for your child. Birthday, anniversary, and other family celebrations have taken place in the dining room. A basement room may have been your own handiwork. When you are thinking about moving, then, it's understandable and right that you consider your emotional ties to your home.

There are practical considerations. Do you still need all the space you have, now that the children have moved out? Are you financially or physically able to maintain a large home? Will you prefer the convenience of living in a smaller or more manageable house during retirement? And, finally, since you are no longer tied to a job in the community, would a different location be better for you? Or would that take you too far away from relatives and friends?

These are some basic questions to ask yourself about your retirement living situation. The remainder of this chapter will raise specific questions and offer information that will help you to make a decision that is right for you.

REMAINING IN YOUR PRESENT HOME

Despite reports of a growing trend toward relocating, relatively few people actually move long distances after retiring. Most people, as they face retirement, think in terms of staying in their present home.

Whether you choose to remain in your present home or to consider a move, you should look at your chosen residence to see how well it meets your physical needs in retirement as well as your social and financial needs.

Home Repairs

Before you retire, special attention should be paid to making home repairs that, if done later, could put a strain on you physically or financially. One wise preventive step would be putting siding on a house that needs frequent painting. Another would be checking your heating, plumbing, and wiring systems. If the roof, yard, driveway, or anything else will need work, you can get an estimate and begin to plan *now* when you want to do it and how to budget for it.

THE WIZARD OF ID — by Brant parker and Johnny hart

Safety

Safety repairs or installations are some of the wisest home investments you make. Here are a few suggestions for making your home safe to live in:

1. Put a nonskid rubber mat or safety strips in the tub and a nonslip mat beside it. Have grab bars in the tub enclosure to hold on to.
2. Keep traffic lanes through all rooms free from hazards to stumble over.
3. Make sure there is adequate lighting ahead of you when you enter a room or go up or down stairs.
4. Never have small rugs at the top or bottom of stairs.
5. Get rid of scatter rugs or anchor them firmly with nonslip mats underneath. Mend all frayed rugs that can trip you.
6. Keep a sturdy stepladder in the house so that you don't have to stand on chairs or tables to reach things.
7. Plan a fire escape route from your bedroom and home. Work out an alternate route just in case.
8. Keep dry chemicals or a carbon dioxide extinguisher for use on electrical and gas fires.
9. Install and periodically check on smoke-detecting devices.
10. If you get up during the night, be sure to turn on a light before moving about the house.
11. Keep emergency phone numbers near the telephone.

Security

Just as it's important for your home to be accident safe, it's equally important for it to be secure. Although many people feel they live in a relatively good area, few, if any, neighborhoods are 100 percent burglary-free. Adequate security at entryways will either put off burglars or delay their entry long enough for them to be noticed or caught.

Here are a few security measures that you can consider including in your home:

Doors

- Replace or reinforce weak wooden or glass doors.
- Install a peephole or a chain latch at the front door.
- Invest in a strong (dead-bolt) lock for the front door.

- Install straight-bolt locks on side and cellar doors.
- Replace outside door hinges with inside ones to prevent easy entry.

Windows

- Reinforce with inside window locks or metal grilles (except those to be used as emergency exits).

About burglar alarms: Unless you live in a high-crime area or are away frequently, having an expensive burglar alarm system installed may not be worth your while. There is a wide range of systems available at various prices, some of which you can install yourself. Talk with your police department and with reputable home security merchants for more information.

Convenience

Although it's difficult to face, our physical abilities decline with age. Gradually, or perhaps suddenly through accident or illness, performing everyday maintenance tasks becomes burdensome. If you plan to remain in your home at an advanced age, consider making changes that will make day-to-day living more convenient, such as installing a half-bathroom on any floor you spend a great deal of time on, placing cabinets and countertops in your kitchen conveniently or installing banisters where there are staircases. Look around for the things that tire you a bit now—later on, you may not be as capable as you are now of handling the strain. Small conveniences can be important in later years and can help continue your independence and self-reliance. Although your home may suit your life-style quite well right now, try to imagine the time when your physical abilities are different—and plan for it!

MOVING TO A NEW LOCATION

Perhaps you are thinking about relocating. *Relocating* can be an exciting prospect. Many people, however, are disappointed with new living situations that they once awaited eagerly, because they failed to plan for them properly. We urge you to look at your own situation carefully and to do as much checking as possible before making a move.

It's important to separate the "popular" moves (the ones everyone seems to think retirees should make) from the ones you feel are right for you. Of course, your own feelings and widely accepted opinions may very well be identical, and that's fine. But if you are thinking of relocating because others tell you that some particular area is a good place to be (and you aren't quite convinced yourself), you could be putting yourself in a very unhappy situation.

Within Your Community

You may feel a strong attachment to your home community. You are comfortable with stores, recreation facilities, churches, libraries, and other institutions that are part of it. You have friends and acquaintances there and a set of activities that you participate in.

New York State Electric & Gas Corporation

33 Ways To Winterize Your Home

16. Change or clean furnace filters monthly.
17. Have a qualified person adjust your heating system.

ADJUSTING YOUR LIVING HABITS

18. Keep the thermostat set at 68 degrees during the day. If this seems too cold for you, try wearing a sweater.
19. Set the temperature back at least 3 degrees at night.
20. If you're going away for a few days, set the thermostat at 60 degrees before you leave.
21. Try lowering the temperature in those rooms you don't spend much time in by adjusting registers, radiators or thermostats.
22. Keep humidifiers at the 30 percent mark or place pans of water on warm air registers or radiators. You'll feel more comfortable at relatively lower temperatures simply by maintaining the right humidity in your home.
23. Cover windows with drapes or curtains.
24. Open your drapes during the day to let the sunshine in and close them at night to keep the cold air out.
25. Try locating your furniture away from cold outside walls and windows.

SOME DO'S

26. Do fix leaky faucets, especially hot water taps.
27. Do use cold water for clothes washing.
28. Do turn off the lights, TV, radio or record player when not needed.

SOME DON'TS

29. Don't permanently fasten windows and doors shut — they may be needed for an emergency.
30. Don't use kitchen appliances to heat your home.
31. Don't use portable heaters as the main source of heat — be particularly cautious with oil or gas space heaters not vented or vented to your chimney.
32. Don't seal off attic ventilation.
33. Don't put insulation over recessed light fixtures.

KEEPING THE COLD AIR OUT

1. Seal all outside doors, including basement doors, with weather-stripping material. In some cases, you can use old carpet strips.
2. Put masking tape around moving parts of windows. Caulk around window and door frames, including those in the basement. You can stop drafts under doors by placing rugs at the bottom.
3. Check pipes entering your home. You can keep the cold air out by packing rags around them.
4. Check light bulb fixtures for air leaks.
5. Put tape over unused keyholes.
6. Make sure unused flue or chimney covers fit tightly.
7. Keep fireplace dampers closed tightly when not in use.
8. Seal your foundation and sill plate with caulking material, insulation or rags.

KEEPING THE WARM AIR IN

9. Install storm windows and storm doors. If you don't have storm windows, you can substitute plastic sheeting but make sure it's tacked tightly all around the edges.
10. Install insulation between warm and cold areas. Begin by insulating the attic floor.
11. Wherever possible, carpet floors. If your attic floor can't be insulated, lay down a carpet.
12. Close off rooms you don't use, particularly those with the biggest windows and the largest outside walls.

MAINTAINING YOUR HEATING SYSTEM

13. Keep your heating system clean.
14. Make sure there is nothing blocking your registers, radiators or baseboard heaters.
15. Keep cold air returns clear.

*Courtesy of New York State Electric and Gas Corporation.

When you are thinking about moving, be sure to distinguish between what you feel about your dwelling and what you feel about your community. It's possible to change homes in retirement without leaving a neighborhood. In fact, as a resident in a particular community, you have a good idea about the housing available—and, if you don't, you may know about others who could help you in your search for a new place. We'll discuss different kinds of dwellings later in this chapter.

Outside Your Community

Here's something important to remember: If you want to move to where the climate is hot because you loved it during your vacation last winter, you would be wise to spend time there during the summer. The same applies to any other popular community that's delightful to visit on vacation. Be sure you feel good about a location's year-round climate and opportunities before you sell your house and pull up roots. Following is a checklist of things to consider when evaluating a new location:

1. How close is the new area to family and friends?
2. Will it be easy to make new friends?
3. Will the climate be acceptable throughout the year?
4. If you want or need to work, how difficult will it be to find a job?
5. Will you be near grocery and department stores, entertainment, and church?
6. Is transportation available: train__bus__taxi__plane__?
7. How close is the nearest hospital?
8. Will you be able to get a family doctor?
9. How high are property taxes? Utility bills?
10. Is the neighborhood zoned to protect your housing investment?
11. Will you be able to pursue your special interests?
12. If you need help from the community or the state with social, economic, health, or other problems, will it be difficult to get it?
13. What special services are available to retired people?

Certain of the questions listed are good to ask yourself regardless of where you decide to live. Naturally, some matters will be more important to you than others. You'll also want to add other factors that don't appear in the chart. Try applying the list you come up with to any community you consider. Talk to people who live there—get their impressions. The investigation of your

retirement living situation should be one of the most thorough ones you ever do, and it will certainly help to ease whatever apprehension and fears you have about money.

Federal tax regulations will allow you to exempt capital gains from the sale of your home on your income tax. You must be fifty-five or older on the day of the sale. In addition, the home must have been your principal residence for three of the last five years before you sell it. For more information and details, contact your local, state or federal tax assistance office.

In many communities homeowners over age sixty-five are entitled to special property tax reductions if their income is below a certain level. For more information about whether or not you qualify, contact the town or county tax assessor, or the Area Agency on Aging where you plan to move or where you now live.

HOUSING ALTERNATIVES

In this section, we'll review the living conditions, responsibilities, and finances involved in various housing opportunities. Remember—what may not have been right for you twenty years ago may be a good choice for you now, and vice versa.

Owning Versus Renting

Most American families live in homes they own. Homeowners are responsible for all the upkeep, maintenance, property taxes, and utility bills of their home. They're free to alter their homes as they please (within zoning regulations). A home mortgage requires a substantial amount of financial security—and a large initial investment. As a retiree, you'll want to consider carefully the effects of inflation on the costs related to homeowning: utilities, maintenance, insurance, and taxes.

When you rent, the responsibilities of maintenance, property taxes, and homeowner's insurance belong to the landlord. You have one major, fairly predictable expense—the rent. But there are also some other expenses, such as some utility payments and renter's insurance. You are also subject to the owner's regulations and specifications. In many cases, these may be written out in a lease, a legal document that obligates both parties to an agreement—and possibly a fixed rent—for a period of time (usually a year or two). However, some leases have clauses or loopholes that may allow a landlord to evict a

THE WIZARD OF ID  by Brant parker and Johnny hart

tenant for a questionable offense. State laws often grant tenants certain rights that may not be specified in a lease. By all means, have a lawyer look at your lease before you sign it if you don't understand it completely.

Since a large down payment is not required, large financial resources aren't necessary for renting (as they are for homeowning). However, you have no investment as you do in a house and, therefore, can't build equity (see page 119).

Private homes vary in how much living and storage space and land they offer. Generally, they afford more room than apartments, and more privacy within a neighborhood. Of course, this varies from setting to setting.

Apartments are located in buildings that contain anywhere from a few to hundreds of units. If your privacy is important to you, this will be a consideration, as will a need to have neighbors close at hand. An apartment also makes the most efficient use of a minimal amount of space. There will be less to clean, but there will also be less room to move around or store things in.

Buying a Smaller Home

You may be able to sell your larger home for more than it would cost to purchase a smaller one. This capital gain, which might be excluded from your gross income (as mentioned previously), could then be invested to produce more retirement income. You would still be able to enjoy the benefits of home ownership but a smaller (and possibly newer) home might provide economies in such expenses as utilities, heating, insurance, and maintenance and repair. Finding a house built on a single level might be another important consideration.

Buying a Two-Family or Multiple Dwelling

The two-family home, also known as a duplex, can make financial sense for a retiring couple. If you purchase the dwelling and live in one of the apartments while renting out the other, the rental income will help cover the mortgage payment; or, if you don't have a mortgage, it could cover other property expenses and still provide extra income. If you are handy at maintenance and repairs, and willing to give up a certain amount of privacy, this kind of dwelling may be ideal for you. Some duplex owners make a arrangement with their tenant by which they reduce the rent in exchange for certain maintenance or repair duties, such as painting, yardwork, etc.

Mobile Homes

Mobile home living has enjoyed a tremendous increase in popularity over the past decade or so, especially among retired people. A mobile home, however, isn't very "mobile." Most of them never move from where they are first parked. Modern mobile homes are from ten to fourteen feet wide (doubles are even more) and range up to seventy-five feet in length. Many of the homes are fully furnished and decorated, including the kitchen.

New mobile homes generally cost less than site-built houses. The purchase price may or may not include the cost of hauling it to your selected site. Usually the quality of the home is directly related to its price. If you are shopping for a mobile home, pay particular attention to construction details with respect to fire, safety, and insulation.

The cost of financing a mobile home is usually higher than for conventional housing. Most financial institutions treat the financing as a personal loan, and interest rates therefore generally run higher than for houses. The mobile home is also likely to depreciate in value during its lifetime. But, unless you let the home fall into a state of disrepair, you'll receive a portion of your investment back, which is a benefit not realized by renters. One other significant advantage is that most states do not levy a real property tax on mobile homes, although they may be taxed as personal property.

Over the years, mobile home parks have improved with the growing popularity of this form of housing. Many parks have attractive landscaping, large lots, driveways, concrete pads on which to put the mobile home, and, in some cases, facilities such as swimming pools, golf courses, and recreation centers. By the same token, because of the growing popularity of this type of living, the cost of renting a space in a mobile home park is constantly increasing. Rental costs should be weighed carefully when comparing the cost of living in a mobile home with the expenses of other kinds of accommodations.

Condominiums and Cooperatives

Condominium and cooperative ownership is gaining in popularity. Most condominiums and cooperatives are apartment buildings, but some vacation and retirement villages operate on the same basis.

For cooperative ownership, you purchase shares in the corporation that owns the cooperative. This allows you to live in a particular apartment, and you make a monthly payment that represents your share of the expenses of operating the complex, including salaries for the managers and personnel, maintenance, real estate taxes, and interest on the mortgage. When you move, you either sell your shares back to the corporation or find someone else to buy your shares from you. An important advantage of this form of ownership is that the value of your shares might increase as the value of the property increases. Also, if you itemize your tax deductions, you can deduct your share of real estate taxes and mortgage interest on your income tax just as if you were a homeowner. Some disadvantages of cooperative ownership are that 1) a decrease in the value of the property reduces the value of your shares, and 2) a high vacancy rate in your cooperative increases your monthly share of expenses: the remaining shareholders must still pay the entire cooperative's expenses.

A condominium is different from a cooperative in that you purchase a particular apartment unit, receive a deed, and own it as you would a house. If you are eligible, you can finance the purchase with a conventional or FHA mortgage. You are usually charged a monthly fee to cover maintenance, repair, and management costs. A condominium is unlike a cooperative in that your apartment receives its own tax assessment and you pay only the taxes on your own unit. As with individual house and cooperative ownership, you can deduct your real estate taxes and mortgage interest on your income tax return.

Shared Housing

Home sharing is one option for reducing the housing costs of older homeowners. Many communities in both urban and rural areas have developed home sharing programs to enable independent senior citizens to remain in the community. Although sharing a home is not a new idea, the recent community involvement is new.

There are two basic forms of community-sponsored home sharing programs. The first is a situation where someone with room to spare shares his or her home with others. This is simply called a "match program." An agency-sponsored program matches homeowners with home seekers through in-depth investigation, counseling, and follow-up. Sharers benefit through alleviated financial burdens, mutual physical assistance, extended independent living, relief from isolation, added safety, and assistance when health fails temporarily, and the list goes on. As a whole, sharers who care act as a "family."

Similar to a match program is a rental referral service, which matches homeseekers with privately owned rental properties. The sharing element is eliminated but through a rental service the concept of decent and affordable housing for the elderly is promoted to the community at large.

Another kind of home sharing can be arranged by a nonprofit community organization that owns or manages several shared housing units within one building. All occupants have equal status and input as to the management of the building. One large renovated home may accommodate anywhere from four to eight individuals.

Home sharing is a housing option that has not yet come into its own. But as housing costs rise and the income of the elderly remains static, the concept of shared living arrangements becomes more appealing.

MULTIGENERATIONAL LIVING ARRANGEMENTS

Tremendous changes in our society have done nothing to lessen the importance and frequency of interaction between older adults and their families. In fact, during times of illness, crisis, or emotionally charged periods (such as major holidays) it is a natural tendency to return to or reflect upon past experiences with our family. This closeness of family ties is revealed in recent studies showing that between 85 and 90 percent of older adults with living children live less than an hour's trip from at least one of the children

Despite the common cry that "the youth of today abandons their parents," family interaction and support of all kinds is continuous throughout our lives, with peaks and valleys particularly in evidence during periods of youth and advanced age. Indeed, many families are actively involved in providing support services (ranging from the emotional support of a phone call or visit to assistance in health care to income assistance and so on) regardless of the older adult's living arrangement, marital status, or other sources of support outside of the family network.

At some time in your life you may have lived under the same roof as your grandparents—or you may have both your children and your parents living with you now. In the future, as your needs, desires, and abilities change, you may consider sharing a household with your children and their families.

Multigenerational or extended family households are not that uncommon. But, in all cases, a great deal of communication, consideration, planning, and work goes into a successful extended family living arrangement.

Here are some of the factors in a successful extended family living situation that you might want to consider.

Privacy

Parents who move in with grown children have been used to the privacy of having their own place. They need to know that they can still maintain some of that privacy in their new location, whether it be a room of their own (with their own belongings) or a portion of the house that is theirs at certain times. The same applies to all other family members.

Freedom

It's important for a retired person to continue to do things outside of the home after moving in with the children. Grown children need the opportunity to get out of the house as well, just as younger children need to maintain activities and friends.

Sharing Household Responsibilities

Problems can arise when a capable older person is denied the opportunity to help out around the house. While an older person may not be able to perform heavy cleaning or maintain a home of their own, he or she can be a real asset in helping out with such things as cooking or light housekeeping.

One of the most common problems in three-generation families begins when one person—often an older parent—offers too much "helpful advice" on the way things should be done. Sometimes, it goes as far as criticizing the way the house is kept, or the children are disciplined. The critic doesn't think there's anything wrong with offering a "suggestion"—but those on the receiving end feel they could do nicely without it, and resent the intrusion.

People often don't realize that "critics" may have little else to do except monitor the work of others. If such persons are given some responsibility of their own, their need to oversee the affairs of others may diminish.

It's especially important for everyone to remember that raising young children is a parent's responsibility, not a grandparent's. This doesn't mean that grandparents can't have a close, loving relationship with their grandchildren. In fact, there's a special relationship that exists between grandparents and their grandchildren that can be hindered when grandparents are expected to duplicate the roles of parents (regarding discipline, in particular).

Older children should also take special care not to take their parents for granted by assuming that they will baby-sit or do certain chores that have not been agreed on in advance.

Living with your parents, or your grown children, can pose some unique problems. Sometimes, however, it's a necessary move, and problems that arise have to be dealt with. If an agreeable arrangement is made from the start and the lines of communication are kept open, it can be not only a satisfactory arrangement but one that adds closeness and new meaning to family bonds.

HOUSING OPTIONS DESIGNED FOR ADULTS

Throughout this chapter, we've discussed housing possibilities that are available to people of all ages. This section will discuss housing that is designed specifically for adults. This category offers several different options designed to meet different needs. Some people enjoy the special social and recreational activities that adult housing provides. Others dislike the "segregation" and lack of day-to-day exposure to people of all ages. The options are presented here for you to consider—either now or in later years, for yourself or for a relative or friend who may want advice in making a decision.

Retirement Communities

The original "retirement villages" were built in outlying areas of popular retirement locations in Florida, Arizona, and California, but today they can be found in the area of most major cities. They cater to older people of different ages, but usually to those aged fifty and older. These communities range from a few hundred residents up to 11,000 or more. Dwellings in retirement communities may be single-family attached or detached houses, duplexes, triplexes or multi-unit buildings. In some cases, dwellings are sold as condominiums or cooperatives. Many of the communities have shopping centers and churches, and some have extra facilities and services such as clubhouses, activity programs, marinas, golf courses and other sports facilities, and resident doctors and other health facilities. Monthly payments for a resident of the retirement community usually include security protection twenty-four hours a day and exterior maintenance and landscaping.

A high morale generally seems to exist among residents of retirement communities and some interesting trends have been noted. One is that retirees who have relocated in a retirement community are usually financially comfortable, socially active, and in good health. Second, because of the residents' bent toward socialization and leisure activities, friendships and patterns of interaction often develop quickly.

Some people report that they are extremely happy living in a retirement community. They find it easy to make new friends, because most if not all of the other residents are in their own age group, and there is a continuous round of social affairs. However, others report that they become dissatisfied with the isolation and lack of contact with other age groups. Before deciding, you should investigate thoroughly. Visit one or more of these communities. Talk with several residents at each. Find out everything you can about the various communities you are considering buying into, and try to determine just what you want out of such a decision. You may be able to rent a unit for a period of time as a trial.

Before you make a decision, be sure to investigate the financial aspects of such a move thoroughly. Be sure you are aware of all regulations, such as limitations on visitations of younger children or grandchildren or banning of pets. Finally, consult your lawyer before signing a contract.

Residential Housing for Elderly

Though retirement communities receive a great deal of attention (especially in the media), older adults are actually more likely to live together in "senior citizen" housing developments within their home community. Such housing units function best when most residents are long-term residents of the area and have intact family relationships and friends, and when the housing unit is located in a stable neighborhood having access to necessary services. These residential facilities are designed for relatively self-reliant and independent retired people. They generally include specially designed safety features such as increased levels of lighting, grab rails, handrails, call systems, nonskid floors, and appliances designed with safety in mind.

Common terms for residential housing include "apartments for the elderly," "retirement hotels," "golden-age villages," and "housing for seniors." Sometimes, condominiums are also built for elderly persons. These condominiums may be much like apartments for the elderly except that the resident purchases rather than rents the unit.

Staff members in residential housing may be limited to a manager, a receptionist and a maintenance staff who generally take care of heavy cleaning of halls, windows, walls, and central activity areas. Extra services such as meals, laundry facilities, and light housekeeping assistance are usually available at an extra charge. Residents may live in individual apartments that include a bathroom, sleeping area, kitchen, and living area. Or they may have studio apartments (where the kitchen, living, and sleeping areas are combined).

Service-Oriented Housing— Adult Care Homes

What minimum services might you expect in "service-oriented" or "personal care" housing for retired people?

Service-oriented housing for older people offers safety features, plus some assistance with daily activities. For example, attendants might help with cleaning, laundry, errands, bathing, and perhaps letter-writing. Help is given only as needed, however. Residents may live in studio apartments or in rooms and often do not have cooking units in their own rooms, because all meals are served in a central dining facility. Some service-oriented housing also offers recreation programs, religious services, and beauty or barber shops.

With this level of supportive service available as needed, residents maintain an independent, self-reliant way of life. In fact, many residents in service-oriented facilities are fairly active in the community, continuing to attend the same events (religious, social, cultural, political, and volunteer) that they did before moving into this housing.

Common terms for service-oriented housing include "homes for the aged," "adult homes," "congregate-care facilities," "rest homes," "domiciliary-care facilities," "sheltered-care for the aging," and "retirement homes." In addition, some "retirement hotels" may be certified to offer this type of service.

Staff members usually include an administrator, attendants, maintenance staff, kitchen staff, and perhaps recreation personnel. This kind of housing and its services are usually regulated by state law.

WHAT ABOUT NURSING HOMES?

Long-Term Care

The phrase "long-term care institution" refers to several different kinds of health facilities. Such institutions are categorized by the degree of care and assistance required by the residents or patients.

The legal words used to denote the level of care provided by long-term care facilities vary from state to state. Generally, however, there are three divisions. The highest level, skilled nursing care, is for those who require around-the-clock nursing supervision but are not so seriously ill as to require hospitalization. The next level, intermediate care, is for those who require some nursing supervision but not on a continuous basis. An institution providing this level of care is sometimes referred to as a "health-related facility." A third level of care is provided by a "domiciliary care facility." At this level, no nursing services are provided, but residents may be assisted in getting about, reminded to take prescribed medication, and helped in arranging transportation for appointments outside the facility.

Many people feel very negative about nursing homes. This may be due in part to the history of such institutions, to personal experience, or perhaps to the recent increase in awareness of living conditions and quality of care in some facilities. In addition, some view nursing homes as places where people are just waiting to die.

A quality long-term care institution, however, is far more than a warehouse for the sick and frail. Many facilities have recreation and education programs, craft shops, entertainment, and other programs designed to help residents and patients stay active and interested in life. Optimally, the institution will work to help residents recover to a stage of independent living.

But, the quality of nursing home care *does* vary a great deal—from excellent to very poor. The first step in learning more about the quality of care and types of services provided by long-term care facilities in your community is to ask your local office for aging about the rating system used in your area. The second step is to visit various facilities for comparison. Ask about the services offered, the cost of care, and how their rating system works. Observe and talk with residents and patients as well as with medical, nursing, and administrative staff.

A Guide to The Right Choice*

No guide can guarantee the right choice of a nursing home. The checklist on the following pages is intended only for your reference and as a convenience when visiting several homes. The most important consideration for any choice is the individual's specific situation. The older patient often has different needs than

---

*Reprinted with permission from *Thinking About a Nursing Home?* published by American Health Care Association, 1200-15th Street, N.W., Washington, D.C. 20005.

the younger resident. The ambulatory patient has other needs than does the bedridden. This guide is for your general reference during personal visits to the homes. The emphasis you place on any question is up to you, but remember that you can't change the patient or resident to fit the home. You must pick the home to fit the resident.

Personnel

Nursing homes provide the services of a variety of full-time and consultant staff specialists. The numbers and kinds of personnel will depend on the needs of the residents.

Nursing personnel are available around the clock. In skilled facilities this twenty-four-hour coverage is provided by licensed nurses. When you tour a facility, look to see if the nursing staff is interacting with patients, answering call signals quickly, and talking with the patients. If special treatments or nursing measures are needed, ask if they will be available.

Activities are provided in all facilities. Ask to speak with the activity coordinator and find out what kinds of individual and group activities they have. Social services may be provided by the facility staff or through an outside agency. Ask about social services.

The dietary department is under the direction of a food service supervisor. A consultant dietician may also be available.

Other specialists may also be on staff or available on a consultant basis: physical therapists, occupational therapists, therapeutic recreators, psychiatric personnel, medical director and consultant pharmacist (both in all-skilled nursing homes), podiatrists and dentists. It is important to find out what specialists you will need and to make sure the facility has them or is able to provide their services.

The overall management of the facility is the responsibility of a licensed nursing home administrator. Other administrative personnel include medical records staff, personnel director, financial director, and building maintenance staffs.

The most important thing to look for in a nursing home is the kind of people who care for the residents. People providing services to people is what nursing home care is all about.

Two Vital Questions

1. Does the home have a current license from the state?
2. Does the administrator have a current license from the state?

If the answer to either of the above questions is "No," do *not* use the home.

Certification, Accreditation and Review

3. If Medicare and/or Medicaid coverage is needed, is the home certified to provide it?
4. Is the home involved with your state health care or nursing home association's Peer Review Committee? (These are professional associations which provide vehicles for the ongoing exchange of knowledge

and experience by staff in order to solve specific and common problems, and promote improved quality standards of care. Ask, if you don't see a notice of participation.

Physical Considerations

5. Location
    a. Pleasing to the patient?
    b. Convenient for patient's personal doctor?
    c. Convenient for frequent visits of family and friends?
    d. Near a cooperative hospital?
6. Accident Prevention
    a. Well lighted inside?
    b. Free of hazards underfoot?
    c. Chairs sturdy and not easily tipped?
    d. Warning signs posted around freshly waxed floors?
    e. Handrails in hallways and grab bars in bathrooms?
7. Fire Safety
    a. Meets federal and/or state codes?
    b. Exits clearly marked and unobstructed?
    c. Written emergency evacuation plan with floor plans posted throughout facility?
    d. Frequent fire drills involving staff and patients?
    e. Exit doors not locked on the inside?
    f. Doors to stairways kept closed?
8. Bedrooms
    a. Open onto hall?
    b. Windows?
    c. No more than four beds per room?
    d. Easy access to each bed?
    e. Drapery for each bed?
    f. Nurse call bell by each bed?
    g. Fresh drinking water beside each bed?
    h. At least one comfortable chair per patient?
    i. Reading lights?
    j. Clothes closet for each patient?
    k. Drawers for each resident's personal items?
    l. Room for a wheelchair to maneuver?
    m. Care used in selecting roommates?
9. Cleanliness
    a. As clean as you set your personal standards?
    b. Free of unpleasant odors?
    c. Incontinent patients given prompt attention?
10. Lobby
    a. Is the atmosphere welcoming?
    b. If also a lounge, is it being used by residents?
    c. Furniture comfortable and attractive?
    d. Plants and flowers?
    e. Wall decorations, bulletin board for activities schedule?
    f. Certificates and licenses on display?
11. Hallways
    a. Large enough for two wheelchairs to pass with ease?

b. Hand-grip railings on the sides?

c. Well lighted?

12. Dining Room

   a. Attractive and inviting?

   b. Comfortable chairs and tables?

   c. Easy to move around in?

   d. Tables convenient for those in wheelchairs?

   e. Food tasty and attractively served?

   f. Adequate time to eat meals?

   g. Meals match posted menu?

   h. Those needing help receiving it?

   i. Area separated from food preparation area?

13. Kitchen

   a. Food preparation, dishwashing, garbage areas separated?

   b. Food needing refrigeration not standing on counters?

   c. Kitchen help observes sanitation rules?

14. Activity rooms

   a. Rooms available for patients' activities?

   b. Equipment (such as games, easels, yarn, kiln, etc.) available?

   c. Residents using equipment?

15. Special-Purpose Rooms

   a. Rooms set aside for physical examinations or therapy?

   b. Rooms available for private visits with family and friends?

   c. Rooms being used for stated purpose?

16. Isolation Room

   a. At least one bed and bathroom for patients with contagious illness when needed?

17. Toilet Facilities

   a. Convenient to bedrooms?

   b. Easy for a wheelchair patient to use?

   c. Sink?

   d. Nurse call bells?

   e. Handgrips on or near toilets?

   f. Bathtubs and showers with nonslip surfaces and handgrips?

18. Grounds

   a. Residents can get fresh air?

   b. Ramps to help handicapped?

   c. Outdoor furniture for use by residents?

   d. Hazardous objects in areas where patients may walk?

Services

19. Medical

   a. Physician available in emergency?

   b. Private physician allowed?

   c. Regular medical attention assured?

   d. Medical records and plan of care kept?

   e. Patient involved in plans for treatment?

   f. Confidentiality of medical records assured?

   g. Other medical services (dentists, optometrists, etc.) available regularly?

20. Hospitalization
   a. Arrangement with a nearby hospital for transfer when necessary?
   b. Is emergency transportation readily available?
21. Nursing Services
   a. Registered Nurse responsible for nursing staff in a skilled nursing home?
   b. Licensed Practical Nurse on duty day and night in a skilled nursing home?
   c. Trained nurses' aides and orderlies on duty in homes providing some nursing care?
22. Pharmacy
   a. All routine and emergency drugs available on a timely basis?
   b. Pharmacist reviews patient drug regimens in skilled nursing facility?
   c. Pharmacist available for staff and patient education and consultation?
23. Therapy Program
   a. Is there a full-time program of physical therapy available under the direction of a qualified physical therapist?
   b. Is therapy available to meet special needs?
   c. Are services of an occupational therapist and speech pathologist available to residents who need these services?
24. Activities Program
   a. Individual patient preferences observed?
   b. Group and individual activities?
   c. Residents encouraged to participate?
   d. Outside trips for those who can go?
   e. Volunteers from the community work with patients?
25. Religious Observances
   a. Arrangements made for patients to worship as they please?
26. Social Services
   a. Social worker available to aid residents and families?
27. Food
   a. Dietician plans menus for patients on special diets?
   b. Are personal likes and dislikes taken into consideration?
   c. Variety from meal to meal?
   d. Meals served at normal times?
   e. Plenty of time for each meal?
   f. Nutritious snacks available?
   g. Food delivered to patients unable or unwilling to eat in dining room?
   h. Help with eating given when needed?
   i. Are warm dishes served warm?
28. Grooming
   a. Assistance in bathing available?
   b. Barbers and beauticians available for men and women?
   c. Does staff encourage neat appearance and give help if needed?

Attitudes and Atmosphere

29. General atmosphere warm, pleasant and cheerful?
30. Staff members show interest in and affection for individual patients? Are courteous and respectful? Stop to chat with patients?

31. Administrator courteous and helpful?
    a. Knows patients by name?
    b. Available to answer questions, hear complaints, or discuss problems?
32. Staff members respond quickly to patient calls for assistance?
33. Personal Preferences
    a. Can residents decorate their own bedrooms?
    b. Can they wear clothes of their choice?
    c. Do current residents present a neat, clean appearance?
34. Visiting hours are convenient for residents and visitors?
35. Civil rights regulations observed?
36. Is there a Patients' Bill of Rights?
37. Are visitors and volunteers pleased with the facility?

Costs

38. Are all services covered in the basic daily charge?
39. If not, is a list of specific services not covered in the basic rate available? (Some homes have schedules covering linen, personal laundry, haircuts, shampoos, pedicures, dental care, etc.)
40. Are payments made in advance returned if the patient leaves the home or dies?

Your Own Share

41. If you are selecting a nursing home for someone else, are you:
    a. Involving this person in the choice of nursing home?
    b. Prepared to ease the patient's transition to the nursing home by being with the patient on admission day and staying a few hours to get the patient settled in?
    c. Ready to visit the patient frequently and to make sure that the patient's friends make similar visits?
    d. Willing to provide the patient with the same amount of love in the nursing home as you would if the patient were able to be at home?

Waiting for Placement

After you have identified a facility for your relative, you may find there is no vacancy. Put your name on the waiting list. In the meantime, check alternatives such as day care, night care, home health agencies, and other community resources that might meet immediate needs. Contact local hospitals regarding services and your local social services agency.

RATING LOCATIONS FOR YOUR RETIREMENT HOME

If you're thinking about relocating in retirement or you'd like to see how your present location "rates," take a look at the following charts, which list locations for retirees by such variables as sunshine and living expenses.

CLIMATE

The Ten Cities with the Highest Percentage of Possible Sunshine—Annual Averages	The Ten Cities that Have the Highest Average Number of Days of Precipitation per Year
1. Phoenix, AZ	1. Juneau, AK
2. El Paso, TX	2. Buffalo, NY
3. Reno, NV	3. Sault Ste. Marie, MI
4. Sacramento, CA	4. Seattle, WA
5. Albuquerque, NM	5. Cleveland, OH
6. Key West, FL	6. Portland, OR
7. Amarillo, TX	7. Burlington, VT
8. Los Angeles, CA	8. Charleston, WV
9. Denver, CO	9. Pittsburgh, PA
10. Salt Lake City, UT	10. Columbus, OH

SOURCE: United States National Oceanic and Atmospheric Administration Comparative Climate Data.

ANNUAL AVERAGE TEMPERATURE
(Selected Cities)

State	City	High	Low
Alabama	Mobile	77.3	57.4
Alaska	Juneau	47.0	33.5
Arizona	Phoenix	85.1	55.4
Arkansas	Little Rock	72.6	49.3
California	Los Angeles	69.2	54.1
	Sacramento	73.2	47.4
	San Francisco	65.1	48.7
Colorado	Denver	64.0	36.2
Connecticut	Hartford	59.6	38.6
Delaware	Wilmington	63.7	44.3
D.C.	Washington	66.7	47.8
Florida	Jacksonville	78.1	58.7
	Miami	83.0	67.9
Georgia	Atlanta	70.3	51.3
Hawaii	Honolulu	83.3	69.8
Idaho	Boise	62.6	39.1
Illinois	Chicago	59.0	38.8
	Peoria	60.5	41.1
Indiana	Indianapolis	62.2	42.4
Iowa	Des Moines	58.3	39.7
Kansas	Wichita	67.6	45.6
Kentucky	Louisville	65.9	45.3
Louisiana	New Orleans	77.7	58.9
Maine	Portland	55.3	34.7
Maryland	Baltimore	65.1	44.8
Massachusetts	Boston	58.7	43.8
Michigan	Detroit	58.3	41.4
	Sault Ste. Marie	49.0	31.0

Continued on page 177

ANNUAL AVERAGE TEMPERATURE (*Continued*)
(Selected Cities)

State	City	High	Low
Minnesota	Duluth	48.1	29.1
	Minneapolis-St. Paul	53.8	34.3
Mississippi	Jackson	77.1	52.8
Missouri	Kansas City	63.5	43.8
	St. Louis	65.8	46.2
Montana	Great Falls	55.9	33.8
Nebraska	Omaha	62.8	40.2
Nevada	Reno	67.0	31.7
New Hampshire	Concord	57.5	33.7
New Jersey	Atlantic City	63.6	43.8
New Mexico	Albuquerque	70.0	43.5
New York	Albany	58.1	37.1
	Buffalo	55.0	39.1
	New York	62.3	46.7
North Carolina	Charlotte	71.2	49.7
	Raleigh	70.4	47.8
North Dakota	Bismarck	53.5	29.3
Ohio	Cincinnati	64.4	43.5
	Cleveland	58.5	40.8
	Columbus	62.1	40.9
Oklahoma	Oklahoma City	71.1	48.7
Oregon	Portland	61.6	43.6
Pennsylvania	Philadelphia	64.2	44.9
	Pittsburgh	60.0	40.8
Rhode Island	Providence	59.0	40.9
South Carolina	Columbia	75.4	51.5
South Dakota	Sioux Falls	56.5	34.2
Tennessee	Memphis	71.7	51.5
	Nashville	70.1	48.7
Texas	Dallas-Fort Worth	76.5	54.4
	El Paso	77.2	49.5
	Houston	79.8	58.0
Utah	Salt Lake City	63.8	38.2
Vermont	Burlington	54.2	34.5
Virginia	Norfolk	68.0	50.6
	Richmond	68.8	46.7
Washington	Seattle-Tacoma	58.8	43.3
	Spokane	57.2	37.3
West Virginia	Charleston	66.0	44.4
Wisconsin	Milwaukee	55.1	36.3
Wyoming	Cheyenne	58.8	33.0
Puerto Rico	San Juan	85.2	72.0

EXPENSE*

These lists show the most expensive and least expensive areas to live for a *retired* husband and wife over the age of 65.

Most Expensive	Least Expensive
1. Anchorage, AK	1. *Nonmetropolitan Areas—South
2. Boston, MA	2. *Nonmetropolitan Areas—West
3. New York, NY	3. *Nonmetropolitan Areas—N. Central
4. Honolulu, HI	4. Orlando, FL
5. Hartford, CT	5. Baton Rouge, LA
6. Washington, DC	6. Atlanta, GA
7. Buffalo, NY	7. Durham, NC
8. Seattle, WA	8. Bakersfield, CA
9. Detroit, MI	9. Nashville, TN
10. San Francisco, CA	10. Austin, TX
11. Philadelphia, PA	11. San Diego, CA
12. Champaign-Urbana, IL	12. *Nonmetropolitan Areas—N. East
13. Cleveland, OH	13. Cincinnati, OH
14. Milwaukee, WI	14. Lancaster, PA
15. Kansas City, MO–KS	15. St. Louis, MO–IL

*Places with populations of 2,500 to 50,000.
SOURCE: United States Bureau of Labor Statistics—Annual Budget for a Retired Couple.

STATE EXPENDITURE

Ten States with the Highest Expenditures per Person	Ten States with the Lowest Expenditures per Person
1. Alaska	1. Florida
2. Hawaii	2. Missouri
3. Wyoming	3. Texas
4. Delaware	4. Tennessee
5. North Dakota	5. New Hampshire
6. New Mexico	6. Indiana
7. Rhode Island	7. Ohio
8. California	8. Georgia
9. Minnesota	9. Nebraska
10. New York	10. Pennsylvania

SOURCE: United States Bureau of the Census: State Government Finances in 1980.

POPULATION 65 YEARS AND OVER BY STATE
(United States Bureau of the Census 1981)

State	Population	State Percentage
Alabama	452,000	11.5
Alaska	12,000	3.0
Arizona	326,000	11.7
Arkansas	320,000	13.9

Continued on page 179

POPULATION 65 YEARS AND OVER BY STATE (*Continued*)
(United States Bureau of the Census 1981)

State	Population	State Percentage
California	2,493,000	10.3
Colorado	255,000	8.6
Connecticut	376,000	12.0
Delaware	62,000	10.3
D.C.	74,000	11.8
Florida	1,759,000	17.3
Georgia	535,000	9.6
Hawaii	81,000	8.2
Idaho	98,000	10.2
Illinois	1,288,000	11.2
Indiana	599,000	11.0
Iowa	394,000	13.6
Kansas	311,000	13.1
Kentucky	418,000	11.4
Louisiana	414,000	9.6
Maine	144,000	12.7
Maryland	409,000	9.6
Massachusetts	739,000	12.8
Michigan	940,000	10.2
Minnesota	490,000	12.2
Mississippi	295,000	11.7
Missouri	658,000	13.3
Montana	87,000	11.0
Nebraska	208,000	13.2
Nevada	72,000	8.5
New Hampshire	106,000	11.4
New Jersey	883,000	11.9
New Mexico	121,000	9.1
New York	2,187,000	12.4
North Carolina	628,000	10.6
North Dakota	82,000	12.4
Ohio	1,199,000	11.1
Oklahoma	382,000	12.3
Oregon	315,000	11.9
Pennsylvania	1,571,000	13.2
Rhode Island	130,000	13.6
South Carolina	300,000	9.5
South Dakota	92,000	13.5
Tennessee	533,000	11.5
Texas	1,412,000	9.6
Utah	114,000	7.5
Vermont	59,000	11.5
Virginia	523,000	9.6
Washington	448,000	10.6
West Virginia	243,000	12.4
Wisconsin	578,000	12.2
Wyoming	38,000	7.8

CRIME

Becoming a crime statistic is something everyone is concerned about. Below are the states with the highest and lowest number of offenses known to the police per 100,000 people. (Includes: violent crimes against persons [murder, forcible rape, robbery, aggravated assault, and so on], and property crimes [burglary, larceny/theft, motor vehicle theft, and so on]).

Highest Number of Crimes Known per 100,000 People	Lowest Number of Crimes Known per 100,000 People
1. Nevada	1. West Virginia
2. Florida	2. North Dakota
3. Arizona	3. South Dakota
4. California	4. Kentucky
5. Colorado	5. Mississippi
6. Oregon	6. Pennsylvania
7. New York	7. Arkansas
8. Michigan	8. Nebraska
9. Washington	9. Maine
10. Delaware	10. Tennessee
11. Alaska	11. New Hampshire
12. Maryland	12. North Carolina
13. Hawaii	13. Idaho
14. New Mexico	14. Indiana
15. New Jersey	15. Virginia

SOURCE: United States Federal Bureau of Investigation, *Crime in the United States,* 1981 Annual.

SITUATIONS TO CONSIDER

Following are a number of situations that pose problems related to the subject of this chapter. There are no right or wrong "answers" to these situations. They are presented simply to stimulate your thinking about retirement and to emphasize certain aspects of retirement planning. It is not necessary to arrive at any particular conclusion about each case.

It's a good idea for couples to review the situations separately and then share their thoughts. If you are single, perhaps you have a friend, relative, or clergyman with whom you can exchange ideas. Discussing situations like these can help to clarify key aspects of retirement planning and will enable you to become more in tune with your feelings and those of others.

Situation 1: Crime in the Area

John must retire from his job in a few years. He lives downtown in a large city and enjoys the activity and diversity the city provides. However, there has been a rash of muggings in his area recently, and his friends are urging him to move to a safer place after he retires. He will have a good income and has maintained good health. John has considered moving outside the city to the suburbs or to a retirement community.

THE WIZARD OF ID   by Brant parker and Johnny hart

Thoughts to Consider

1. How might the activities provided in a retirement community differ from those in a city? What adjustments might John have to make?
2. Do you think the suburbs (especially those close to a large city) are any safer than the cities themselves?
3. What kinds of things might John do to feel safer? (Study karate? Get a watchdog?)
4. What do you know about "Neighborhood Watch" communities? Is there one in your area?

Situation 2: Physical Limitations and Housing

Virginia recently had a friend over for dinner who could only get about in a wheelchair. She noticed how even a simple thing like the one step between the dining and living rooms presented a problem. This made Virginia think about how her home might one day present problems for her should her arthritis worsen. What kinds of things in her home should Virginia be looking at?

Thoughts to Consider

1. What features might be valuable to add to your home regardless of physical condition? (Grab bars in the bathroom, nonslip rugs, nonslip surfaces in the bathtub, etc.)

    (1)   (6)
    (2)   (7)
    (3)   (8)
    (4)   (9)
    (5)   (10)

2. What about features related to:
    Climbing—Stairs to basement, upstairs, outdoors, etc.
    Reaching—Cabinets, light bulbs, etc.
    Pushing—Heavy furniture, tight doors, etc.

3. Which of the things we mentioned can you do something about, and which are you stuck with?

    Can Change   **Can't Change**
    (1)   (1)
    (2)   (2)

Can Change	Can't Change
(3)	(3)
(4)	(4)
(5)	(5)

Situation 3: Sunbelt Retirement

For several years, Edna and Jerry have been planning to sell their house and move to Florida after they retire. Six months ago, they bought a small house in one of their favorite vacation spots. Now, with retirement three months away, Edna is wondering if the purchase was a wise one. She's not looking forward to the hot summers, and she'll miss the northern city she's lived in all her life and her friends there. However, seeing how enthusiastic her husband has been about Florida and their "new life" there, she has been afraid to say anything about her second thoughts. What should Edna do?

Thoughts to Consider

1. Do you think Edna's fears are realistic (understandable)? Do you think they could be easily forgotten?
2. What might prevent Edna from talking to her husband about her concerns?
3. What are the obstacles, financially, to keeping two homes for a while? How might they be overcome?
4. What problems might arise if they made the move and she wasn't happy?
5. What do you think Jerry's reaction to this will be?

Situation 4: Moving Within the Community

For thirty years Bob and Janice have worked hard to make their home a place of comfort and beauty in the little college town in which they live. Their adult children are living in other parts of the country. Bob's recent heart attack prohibits him from doing heavy work. He will retire in five years from the college faculty with an income adequate to meet their needs. Even though they enjoy their home and the friendship of neighbors, Janice is beginning to wonder if they should sell and move to an apartment or a small, low-upkeep home. How can they meet their needs and their desires too?

List some of the pros and cons of selling a larger home and moving to a smaller one:

Good   Bad

Situation 5: Co-op or Condominium?

Joan will retire in a year and plans to sell her large older home. She has an opportunity to purchase at a "bargain price" a condominium apartment from a friend who is moving south. She has also found that there is an apartment available in a nearby, desirable cooperative housing facility. Joan feels that the co-op may be a better investment than the condominium. What can she do to make the best choice?

Possible Approaches

1. Buy into the co-op; her investment may increase.
2. Buy the condominium; her investment is more secure and monthly expenses will be more stable.
3. Rent an apartment and put her money in an income-producing investment.
4. Start a thorough investigation of condominiums and co-ops, but don't do anything right now.
5. Get advice from a lawyer.

Thoughts to Consider

1. What are the differences between a co-op and a condominium?
2. What might a vacancy in the co-op do to monthly costs?
3. When shouldn't a "bargain" be jumped at? Would she be making a mistake by hesitating?
4. What could a lawyer help Joan with?
5. What must Joan do for herself?
6. Have you begun to investigate your retirement housing options?

Where we live is a critical matter in our lives. It's important, then, that your decision about retirement housing take into consideration many factors—financial, emotional, and practical. In this chapter, we have discussed some of the housing options you have as you approach retirement. By considering them now, you can plan for the kind of future you want.

REFERENCES AND RESOURCES

Adelmann, Nora E. *Directory of Life Care Communities: A Guide to Retirement Communities for Independent Living.* New York: H.W. Wilson, 1981.

Dickinson, Peter. *Retirement Edens: Outside the Sunbelt and Sunbelt Retirement: The Complete State by State Guide to Retirement in the South and West of the United States.* New York: E.P. Dutton, 1981.

Guide to Housing Security. Washington, D.C.: Action for Independent Maturity (1909 K St., N.W., 20006).

Guide to Retirement Living. Chicago: Rand McNally & Co. (P.O. Box 7600, 60680), 1973.

Heintz, Katherine M. *Retirement Communities: For Adults Only.* New Brunswick, N.J.: Center for Urban Policy Research, 1976.

Horn, Linda, and Elma Griesel. *Nursing Homes: A Citizen's Action Guide.* Boston: Beacon Press, 1977.

Irwin, Robert. *The $100,000 Decision: The Older American's Guide to Selling a Home and Choosing Retirement Housing.* New York: McGraw-Hill, 1981.

Lawton, M. Powell, and Sally L. Hoover. *Community Housing Choices for Older Americans.* New York: Springer Pub. Co., Inc. (200 Park Ave. South, 10003), 1981.

Rabizadeh, Masoud. *Housing for the Elderly.* Eugene, Or.: University of Oregon Publications (320 Susan Campbell Hall, University of Oregon, 97403), 1982.

Scholen, Kenneth, and Chen Yung-Ping. *Unlocking Home Equity for the Elderly.* Cambridge, Mass.: Ballinger, 1980.

Smith, Bert K. *Looking Forward: New Options for Your Later Years.* Boston: Beacon Press, 1982.

Sumichrast, Michael. *Where Will You Live Tomorrow? The Complete Guide to Selecting a Retirement Home.* Homewood, Ill.: Dow Jones-Irwin, 1981.

Woodall's Retirement Directory. Highland Park, Ill.: Woodall, annual.

Woodall's Sunbelt Retirement Directory. Highland Park, Ill.: Woodall, annual.

Worley, H. Wilson. *Retirement Living Alternatives USA: The Inside Story.* Clemson, S.C.: Columbia House Pub. Corp., 1982.

Your Retirement Home Repair Guide, Your Retirement Housing Guide, and *Your Retirement Moving Guide.* Washington, D.C.: American Association of Retired Persons (1909 K St., N.W., 20006).

A Final Word

Congratulations, you have completed the first and largest step in securing your future. In the previous seven chapters we have outlined the major components of successful preretirement planning. The successive steps you take in fulfilling your retirement plan will be natural and sensible according to your needs.

You are now armed with the one clear and proven weapon we have for combating the problems encountered by today's "aging society"—preretirement education. Most of the economic, social, and personal problems facing older adults today could have been avoided or lessened considerably if proper preparation for aging had been an integral part of our basic education. But it wasn't until the early 1970's that we as a nation came to view preretirement education as an important and necessary part of life.

As the concept of preretirement education develops in the classroom, in industry, and in the public image, we will see enormous changes (and strides made) in the overall status of older Americans. Many of the economic and social problems of today can and will be overcome; and as we age, we will take our rightful place as valuable and contributing members of society.

We hope you have been motivated to do three things as a result of reading this book. These are:

First, secure your future and the future of those you love.

Second, spread the word about the long-range benefits of formulating a plan for retirement as early as possible.

Third, help us to destroy the myths of aging and replace them with truth and understanding.